HAPPINESS
and HAPPY MONEY

Rafael D. Kasischke

HAPPINESS
and HAPPY MONEY

Bibliographic information from the German National Library:
The German National Library lists this publication in the
German National Bibliography; detailed bibliographic data can
be accessed online at http://dnb.dnb.de.

Publisher: BoD · Books on Demand GmbH, In de Tarpen 42,
22848 Norderstedt
Print: Libri Plureos GmbH, Friedensallee 273, 22763 Hamburg

ISBN: 978-3-7693-1480-9

This book is for the many human souls
dedicated to those who do not yet live in ease
and looking for joy in life,
of laughter and lightheartedness.

May the light shine on these people
and bring them happiness.

Contents

Foreword

Radiant, joyful, golden LIGHT flows to the people. Golden LIGHT shines around them. People feel LOVE. They feel secure. They feel comfortable. They are happy. A deeply felt HAPPINESS and JOY surrounds them. They are touched by this light. It fills their HEARTS. They feel the LOVE and connection with something greater – the universal energy.

Light – Love – Ease – Peace – Freedom – Mindfulness – Compassion – Gratitude – Recognition – Truth – Trust – Respect – Heat Opening – Intuition – Dancing – Laughing – Cheerfulness – Exuberance – Serenity – Carefreeness – Inner Wealth – Inner Values – Inner Contentment surround these people. They feel happily understood and at home in their hearts. Full of joy, they embrace their family, neighbors, and community.

And this cheerfulness is noticed by others. They come and want to understand what is happening here: a great transformation in people – from dejection, fear, and suffering to opening of hearts, receiving golden light, and feeling joy and happiness. More and more people are coming. They, too, receive love, golden light, and joy. A chain reaction begins.
Much more people are drawn and want to experience this miracle. From suffering, fear, sorrow, pessimism, and anxiety about the future, decline and chaos transform into calm, confidence, optimism, new beginnings, joy, ease, and thus happiness.

How is this possible? How could this happen? Who initiated it? Is this fiction? Is it just this moment? Or does this new awakening endure? It is not fiction. It is not a dream. It is the near future. We make people happy. We lift them out of their dreary lives and surround them with a halo that shines deep into their being, reaching their body cells and feelings, turning them from dark to golden.

Because our consciousness has grown overnight. And with our consciousness, our body, mind, and emotion cells have expanded. Our traumas, our past experiences, and our current hopeless situation have disappeared overnight. A golden glow has come over the people who were open and ready for it. And now these people are infecting others. They too want to taste this nectar of bliss. And they, too, are filled with the new, with love, joy, and gratitude. And they, too, receive the golden – the halo. All of this is not a vision but the near future. This feeling of happiness among people is at the doorstep.

Every day we read about the topic of happiness in the media. There is even a country ranking of the happiest people. The Nordic countries like Finland, Denmark, Iceland, Sweden, and Norway top the World Happiness Report 2024. But have we become happier because of the media and the publication of the happiest countries? No. It sometimes makes people more unhappy because they think: How can others be happy, and not me?

We can all be happy. And that's what this book is about. However, as mentioned earlier, the switch to happiness is coming soon. It has not happened yet. Until then, we must still follow the conventional path to inner happiness. And that path is sometimes a bit thorny. It is certainly a process that we learn through life's experiences. But fundamentally, we are happy from birth. After all, we are blessed to be born into this world and have the opportunity to experience the richness of life, i.e. its experiences.

As children, we laugh the most. Later, we forget how to do that. We need to remember those carefree times and reactivate the laughter and joy – from the heart. And we must encourage others to follow the same path. In doing so, peace and joy enter our lives and the world. It is about regaining the happiness we experienced as children but then lost.

Because every human being – all of us – wants to be happy. Are you happy? Why? By what means? Every day or only rarely? How does your happiness manifest itself? Do you want to know how to be constantly happy or even happier? Some people are happy today and unhappy tomorrow – so unstable.

There are many books, advice, and suggestions. I've read some to gain the wisdom of other authors. But few have convinced me. Why not? Many approach it scientifically. The magic word is positive psychology. Or they are pseudo-spiritual with great advice.

I approach the topic differently, from a practical point of view.
To me, happiness is a process you can't learn overnight.
Like everything in life, it has its two sides. We live in duality:
Day – Night, Light – Shadow, Joy – Sorrow, War – Peace, Positivity – Negativity.

To reach happiness, we must go through experiences – both positive and negative. It's best not to know beforehand what it's all about. You just walk the path – whether it leads to prosperity or to the abyss. It will reveal itself. And if, for example, you have gone the path towards the abyss and come out again, then you have made one of the experiences and reached the goal. You can practically check that experience off your list.

And so, there are many experiences that contribute to happiness. But first, we must go through them. If you've taken the path to prosperity, it doesn't mean you will never experience the abyss again. It may still meet you on your journey. And then suddenly, joy and lightness turn into heaviness, sorrow, and suffering. Why? We identify with our body, our history, our parents, our job, our wealth instead of viewing everything from a distance and with wisdom.

Introduction

Many people are searching for happiness, joy in life, and a sense of purpose. They already have enough worries, fears, and doubts. This book is intended to inspire joy and reflection about life. I gladly welcome any recommendations and suggestions.

I have given several talks on happiness: "How do I bring serenity and joy into my life? Happiness & Money" are the titles of my talks. Or: "How do I become cheerful, carefree, and fearless? Many people are under stress, earning money, worrying about the future, dealing with family problems, depression. Rafael knows these issues from his own experience. Through his inner transformation, he has become a cheerful, fun-loving person. Would you like to become like this too?"

I also offered Swiss and German companies to make their employees happy. I was told that all their employees are happy and that they have enough in-house professionals for that. Of course, I am very pleased that this topic has reached all companies and that their employees are now happy. Naturally, I had to smile at these responses. In our world today, only a few are truly happy and full of joy (beyond joy).

"Why are Colombians happier than Swiss people?" I asked a Colombian doctoral student at the University of St. Gallen. He focuses his research on preserving the cultural and ecological heritage of Colombia's indigenous communities, as well as on mechanisms of mediation and dialogue within the United Nations. He has lived in Switzerland for several years and knows the differences between the two countries very well.

His answer was: the Colombian people possess internal gifts that are hidden from the Swiss and other Western nations. It is the joy beyond, the inner happiness, the laughter, the jokes, the spark (chispa = Spanish), the mischievousness, slyness, impishness, and playfulness (piardia = Spanish).

Where does this power come from? From a source to which everyone actually has access, but many have forgotten or suppressed tapping into this source and feeling into an energy that cannot be touched. Indigenous peoples have access to this source. Harmonization is their magic word – harmonization among people (and not individualization) and harmonization with nature. I call it spirituality.

I want to inspire and sensitize people to find the inner gold – joy, lightness, childlike wonder, love, and wisdom – within themselves and to become happy.

My goal is to make the world a better place and bring happiness into it. The challenge is to change people's mindset and attitude and detach from ego and money.

On August 24, 2024, I met a couple from India on Bahnhofstrasse in Zurich. A young man held a sign in his hand: "Positive People Wanted." The Indian couple and I approached the young man with the sign at the same time. We discussed positive people and happiness. "How do we find happiness?" asked the Indian. "By doing something for other people that touches our heart as the giver and the heart of the recipient, without expecting anything in return – purely out of altruism." Of course, we may receive something in return. But not in the usual way – a large sum of money. Greed and profit maximization are no longer in demand. I am writing about this in Chapter 7.

What has touched my heart, and what am I grateful for?
I am grateful for my life. I am writing about this in Chapter 6. And I am grateful for the experiences I have had in my life. Because of these experiences, I have become happy. Today, I have far less material than before. But today, I have so much – in knowledge, wisdom, experiences, and my talents and gifts. Every day, I meet new people, give them joy, sunshine, and golden light, and take away their fear.
This is a wonderful gift that touches my heart, and for which I thank the greater whole.

Do you need to have great material wealth to be happy? I had wealth – with a very large house of my own in the best location in Miami/Florida. A large park-like driveway with a fountain adorned the front yard. In the backyard was a magnificent garden with a large pool, adjacent to the golf club of the famous

Biltmore Hotel, with a view of Par 3 from the upstairs bedroom. Two cars in the garage. The children at a private school.

Around us were the most beautiful villas with the richest people of Miami, and constant invitations and celebrations. Professionally, I was successful – representing the interests of a Swiss bank in Latin America. So, you can be happy like that. And I was.

But later – when that external glamour was taken away from me – I became even happier. This is a story about me and others, about true inner happiness.

We can learn: Life is not about accumulating possessions, but about evolving.

We might ask: Does what I am doing help me evolve? Am I helping others to evolve, or to reduce their suffering and confusion? Especially in our crazy world today, full of unpredictable things and actions taking place in people's minds – whether they are on the world stage or in refugee camps – the distress and suffering among people is great. We may lend them our ear. And we may offer them confidence, light, and love. By doing so, we grow.

And development includes not only giving and gratitude but also forgiveness. Throughout our lives, we are confronted with many things unjustly. And we ourselves confront others – as children and teenagers, first our parents with many unpleasant words, accusations, or reproaches, and later, of course, other people in our environment.

We should forgive these negative thoughts, words, and accusations towards ourselves and forgive others for their actions towards us. This tool of forgiveness is one of the most important on the path to happiness. I forgive the perpetrator who did this or that to me or my children. And I forgive myself for what I have done to others.

We humans are both: victims and perpetrators (aggressors). But there is another position: the liberator, the savior, the redeemer. In life, we move from one role to the other: from victim to aggressor, and then to savior.

We must try to break out of this triangular relationship and view the roles from a distance. We must become the hero or heroine – the storyteller – not the victim of a story. We know, we are not our genes. Only 10% of us are defined by our genes.

If we see ourselves as guests on this planet and take ourselves out of our identification, becoming observers of the whole theater and viewing it from a distance, we will be calm and cheerful and find peace of soul.

My mission: to make you, dear reader, happy – to bring you joy, love, cheerfulness, and lightness, and to relieve you of the weight of your burdens.

Immerse yourself in this new energy. You will experience yourself and the world around you with new eyes.

1. Chapter: What is Happiness?

Happiness, joy, and laughter are part of the fundamental nature of being human. Children are naturally happy. Because they know no fear. Because they haven't yet experienced negative events in life (job loss, financial loss, relationship loss, bankruptcy, fraud, corruption, etc.).
They are carefree and adventurous. They embrace the adventure of life. They want to discover and experiment – to test their own limits and those of others. They trust. They want to play and have fun. They want to surprise and be surprised. They want to be delighted. Curiosity, lightness, and zest for life shine in their eyes.

And we adults – what do we want? We also want to experience adventures, test our limits, have fun, and play – with money, life, and "fire." We burn ourselves and start over. When it really hurts, we stop.

As adults, we want to have experiences similar to those of children, but on a completely different level of awareness. We have already had certain negative experiences. As a result, we laugh less, are less carefree, and dive into life less readily than children do. This results in less happiness compared to children. Yet, we want to try to regain this – to revitalize it – to reconnect with our inner child. To view life through the eyes of a child, become playful, open our senses, and begin to laugh heartily again.

What needs to happen to regain this carefree, childlike joy, this trust in the divine? It requires a new perspective on life. We experience a new lightness. Joy for life spreads. A new life begins.

> *"If you dare something, your courage grows.*
> *If you hesitate, your fear grows."*
> Mahatma Gandhi

But first, the question: What is true happiness? It is the connection of my mind to my heart and my soul. Everything is harmoniously connected. No part wants to be more important than the other – not the mind (and potentially the ego), nor the heart or the soul. The soul is the most important part of this trio – this connection. Because the soul is integrated into us even before birth. It is the foundation of our being. It sets the tone.

We believe our mind sets the tone. No, that's not true. The soul determines our path – even if the path is rocky, winding, and perhaps not ethical or moral. The soul wants to experience this path too. And so, we walk this path – we are allowed to – so that the soul can gain this experience.

And what role does the heart play in this trio? The heart is the bridge between mind and soul. The heart tells us what is right and wrong. The heart is the measure – the compass. When my heart is pure, it shines and feels good, then my mind and soul are in harmony. All three feel good. And then I am in happiness. And then I am in spiritual, emotional, and mental health.

But I cannot achieve this at a young age, because before I reach this state of inner happiness, I must go through the experiences my soul wants to live. The mind plays along with all the games.

Because in us humans, there is polarity: good and evil, positivity and negativity. When it comes to negative actions, the heart is simply switched off. It welcomes the positive ones and rejoices. It must be added that this trio is connected to the great soul – universal energy – which is another reason for our feeling of happiness. We feel guided, understood, and protected.
Happiness, then, is a feeling. We feel light, buoyant, joyful, carefree. We feel like we could uproot trees. Our endorphin levels (our joy hormones) reach their peak.

> *"The greatest attraction there is,*
> *is the world within you. Take a look at it."*
> Kurt Tucholsky

However, I feel that many people in the world are not happy – both the poor and the rich. The difference between poor and rich is money. The poor can sometimes be even happier than the rich. Because this feeling resides in their hearts, and they radiate joy and happiness. Their eyes are the mirror of their soul. They live in the "now," not in the past or the future.
The poor do not always want "more and more," as is often the case with the rich. Yet the poor need the same things as the rich: a roof over their head, food and drink, as well as education and health.

The rich believe they are happy because they can afford many things. But wealth and possessions can also be a burden. One must manage them, grow them, and control them. Some have a fear of loss and worry. And then comes the question at the end of life: To whom will we pass on our wealth? Will our children and grandchildren handle it well? I have lived among the rich. I know their worries, fears, and thoughts.

Curt Engelhorn, former patriarch of the pharmaceutical industry (Boehringer Mannheim), once said: *"My whole life I have been searching for warmth and recognition. Throughout much of my life, I have failed."* He was a neglected child, traumatized by his parents' divorce. He became the father of neglected children, traumatized by his affairs. He belonged to the world of great wealth. Yet he was lonely and poor.

This is the case for many. But very few open their hearts and say what they feel. Powerful, successful men are often hardened. They have a strong outward character, but their soul withers away. It functions as long as the external life works. Then comes a desperate emptiness.

Aristotle Onassis: *"A rich man is often just a poor man with a lot of money."*
Paul Getty: *"Having money does not free one from worries about money."*

In October 2024, I had the privilege of being invited to an international event in India (Mt. Abu/Rajasthan). It was a spiritual retreat focused on self-awareness and consciousness of body, mind, and soul.

At this retreat, I was able to deeply connect with myself – to listen and feel, to strengthen my inner self, so that I can spread happiness to the world in the future. The messages I received and the conversations with many participants during the week-long retreat were so inspiring, healing, and enlightening that it becomes easier and easier for me to accept and walk my path in the world.

I had the opportunity to meet 70 people from different countries: South Africa, Kenya, Ghana, Mauritius, Seychelles, India, Japan, Indonesia, Malaysia, Vietnam, Dubai, Bosnia, England, Italy, Spain, Brazil, Trinidad, Canada, and the USA.

I asked each participant for their opinion on the sense of happiness among the population in their respective countries. The answers were very similar: people are focused on material things. Many are therefore under stress. Outwardly, they seem happy. But it is only an appearance – not true reality.

Already during the four-hour drive from Ahmedabad to Mt. Abu in a taxi that I shared with a young journalist from Dubai, we talked about happiness in Dubai. Of course, people there are happy, she said, because they only see the material side of life. They don't know the connection with nature and spirituality.

I received the same answer shortly before from Saudi Arabia, at a real estate fair in Munich.

Because of our material world, the true, deeply felt sense of joy and happiness has been lost. Yet many yearn for it. This means that all of us who possess this deep-seated feeling within us are called upon to bring it into the world and make people truly happy from the heart, to bring light and joy.

As an example, I want to mention Japan in response to my question about happiness. The answer comes from a university professor from Hiroshima, Dr. Fuyuko Takita.
On the topic of happiness, she told me about the three stages in Japan:
Ancient Japan: Due to the old Japanese national religion of Shintoism, people experienced more true inner happiness, as the main principles of Shintoism are the importance of purity, harmony, and respect for nature. Ancient Japanese were more strongly connected to the divine and were thus, in the truest sense of the word, happier.

Modern Japan: As Japan modernized like the Western world, the Japanese economy flourished. And people in Japan began to become very wealthy in material terms. While they enjoyed material abundance, the people, especially the younger generations in Japan, started experiencing a stronger separation from the spiritual world. Just like in the Western world, with increasing material satisfaction and abundance, many Japanese began to focus on competition and the pressure to succeed. This led to even more emptiness inside them. They began to suffer from anxiety and depression.

Lack of Spirituality and Increased Individualism: Japan is considered a Buddhist country, however very few practice Buddhism, and many people have no connection to the divine or learn nothing about spirituality in this country. Many younger generations are becoming more individualized, increasingly detaching from society and the community. Since many do not possess the wisdom of spiritual identity – "Who am I?" – many people in this country wear masks, trying to please others and not living their true-life purpose.
Due to this lack of spiritual wisdom, many have lost the purpose of life – a highly interesting concept of Japanese happiness.

(Dr. Fuyuko Takita / University of Hiroshima)

I would like to add that in Japan, emotions are rarely shown. They are suppressed. The goal is to avoid emotions – especially negative ones – and to save face. Here's an example:
A very large company had a new office building constructed – with fitness and relaxation rooms, among others, as well as a room that was completely separate and had thick walls. It was meant for employees to release their pent-up aggression, anger, etc., in this room. However, it turned out that no employee used this room.

This means: Japanese people hold on to their emotions and do not express them. It has to do with their culture – respect for elderly people and not showing true, honest feelings.
Can a person become happy if they do not express their true feelings? And isn't the feeling of connectedness to something greater - a universal energy - important in order to feel happy?

The emotional state is quite different in the southwestern countries of the world—in Spain, Italy, and Latin America. There, people show their emotions. But does that make them happier? Not necessarily, unless they are connected to a source, as mentioned before.

In Mt. Abu I met Christina Carvalho-Pinto for the third time at the retreat. She is a film producer from Sao Paulo who is internationally recognized in the field of transformative media that combines creativity and consciousness. She writes about the sense of happiness among Brazilians:

"Brazil is a gigantic melting pot of peoples and cultures from all parts of the world: from our native indigenous people to Germans and Japanese, from Africans to Chinese, from Italians to Portuguese, from Spanish to French and Dutch, and many others. The result of this fascinating mix is a Brazilian soul with unique characteristics. Joy, flexibility, human warmth, creativity, and resilience live within us in a perceptible and original way.
Now, are we happy? The most recent research shows that 83% of Brazilians say, 'Yes, I am happy.' On the other hand:

How profound is this response in a country, in a world so challenged by shadows?

Yes, our Brazilian nature is joy and happiness, but in companies, people at all hierarchical levels suffer from burnout, depression, and other mental disorders. Depression, anxiety, and suicide are increasing unexpectedly among children and teenagers.

Across the world, the most powerful decision-makers have ignored (and continue to ignore) all warnings about climate change, and so we are now witnessing the era of climate crisis.

Even though, I am happy, and I know that you, Rafael, are happy too. We – and so many others – look at this time as a great opportunity to spread happiness. It is not a symptom of alienation. It is a pure reminder of where we come from and to whom we belong. Soul consciousness leads us to feel and share what people need most: love and peace, the true path to happiness."

Of course, we cannot generalize about the population in every country. Naturally, there are exceptions who exist in a deep inner state, at a higher level of consciousness. For instance, at our retreat, there was a monk from Durban, South Africa, who has developed deep inner knowledge over many years and is very content with himself and the world around him.

Additionally, a very wise and experienced journalist at the retreat drew my attention to an example from Nepal: Matthieu Ricard.

He is a Buddhist monk, author, and photographer known for his happiness. He gave up his scientific career to practice Tibetan Buddhism. He now lives in the Himalayas.

We do not need to travel so far or so high to become happy. It is enough to transform our inner self. The time for this is ripe.

"Happiness" is not just a word, but a new movement in the world – a world filled with worries, fears, suffering, and grief. The world, or rather its people, needs happiness, hope, and a vision of a new, more beautiful world – full of peace, deep understanding, insight, and awareness.

What is Happiness? Happiness is the connection with nature, the loving bond with other people, the connection of oneself to a higher power. My conversation with the director of the Global Hospital in Mt. Abu confirmed this. When we look at life – our life – with new eyes and deep understanding, we feel happy, even if life were to end.

What Does It Take to Achieve Happiness? Meditation – diving into our true self and receiving messages, insights, signposts, and solutions to the issues in our lives.
Furthermore, we must express our feelings rather than hold them back or hide them. By doing so, we free ourselves from our inner constraints.

We should also approach others, build connections with them, and in the future, create a community. People in many underdeveloped countries are somewhat happier because they have a circle of acquaintances among their peers and are in close contact. This is less common in highly developed countries. Nowadays, there is social media, but it does not replace the personal and emotional connection between people.

"And we must direct our thoughts in a positive direction. Plant the seed of positive thoughts. Let the seed grow. Then positive things will come to light."

2. Chapter: Reflections on Cheerfulness, Laughter, and Lightness

How beautiful it is to see and observe cheerful people. They are calm, relaxed, and glide through the day with ease. My heart rejoices every time.

Cheerfulness is a fundamental view of the world, of ourselves, and of others, of life and death. It's about our attitude toward life. Cheerfulness does not deny the seriousness of the world. It takes it in and transforms it. "Humor is simply a funny way of being serious," Peter Ustinov once said. And Sigmund Freud: "There are forks in the road of life where one can decide not to take the route of worry but of laughter, or better yet, of smiling. Making the right decision, choosing not to suffer from life, is a great achievement."

Humor is the ability to free oneself from the traumas one experienced as a child through parents. One looks down at oneself from an elevated position and smiles lovingly at oneself—at one's own foolishness, mistakes, and actions. For the dominant, fear-inducing pressure of the father was a trauma for the child. For these and other reasons, many people have lost their cheerfulness and their smile. It is almost like a talent to regain this new perspective on the world and oneself.

Our thinking is focused on possession and consumption. Only when we let go of our fixation on possessions and the fear of losing them, and adopt a new perspective on life, can a bit more cheerfulness arise. But in us still lies the message from our parents and society: Be diligent and achieve a lot. The message was never: Be cheerful!

Cheerfulness cannot be taken as a pill, bought on Amazon, or booked as a seminar. And reading a self-help book isn't enough.

In ancient philosophy, there is the term "eudaimonia," often translated as happiness, which is not quite right. All disputes among ancient philosophers revolved around the path to "eudaimonia." An important role on this path was played by peace of mind. Should one dedicate oneself to work, pleasure, or modesty? Seneca said: "Lower your expectations of life; do not cling to life. It is better to laugh at life than to weep over it. So, no self-overburdening, being free of expectations, being lenient with others, and oneself."

How can we manage to be cheerful in real life—to create lightness within ourselves? Answer: We don't always have to laugh. But we can smile and practice everyday kindness, listen to others. And we can show others our interest, curiosity, attentiveness, goodwill, and comfort. Thus, we can see life for what it also is: a game.

What matters are smiling, being kind, accepting things, transformation, lightness, mildness, kindness, and equanimity.

The following are some thoughts on happiness:

1. **Life consists of joy and happiness**. But do work and money lead to happiness? No! For 2,000 years, parents and society have told us to learn and study to get a job and make a living. For 2,000 years, the church and all religions have taught us to work to be content. But no one has told us how to be happy in life. Learning in school, studying at universities, and working in a job do not make us happy. And earning money does not make us happy either. What makes us happy? The answer is in our heart. It is time to change our consciousness and beliefs and embrace happiness—in life, at work, and with money.

2. **We are on earth to have experiences**—our soul wants both good and not-so-good experiences. We are not here to cling to money and ego. We may now let go of this attachment and embrace joy. And joy comes from a source deep within us. We are connected to a source that is always there and nourishes us. Let us feel this source.
If we have nothing left in life (all material things taken from us), something remains that is far more valuable than anything material. It is our connection to the source. And that brings us joy. Some people in poorer countries carry this wisdom within them. In their faces, love and joy can be seen.

3. **Can we buy true cheerfulness and joy with money?**

Can we buy protection against cancer or dementia with money? Can we take money with us when we pass away? The answer is: No! We need to rethink our previous focus on money.

Our attachment to material things is no longer appropriate. And the belief that "money makes you happy" even less so. We need to find the joy of life, lightness, and carefree nature within us, not outside.

4. **When we are cheerful and joyful** (and not fearful), **all our past negative actions are healed**, especially our body cells, which may be afflicted by cancer cells. The negative cells are rejected, and new, positive cells grow. Joy is the greatest transformative power. It heals everything.

5. **Fear is the biggest obstacle in today's world and, at the same time, a challenge for each of us**. Our thoughts constantly revolve around fear—fear of losing our job or social status, fear of failure or financial loss. We must replace fear with love. When we are in joy, which is synonymous with love, we have no more fear.

6. **Many people worry about different things**. These worrisome thoughts determine our feelings. A new perspective—a new view—helps us move away from those thoughts. Transformation happens! We must therefore pay attention to our thoughts— have only positive thoughts, avoid news, media, stress, addiction, ego, and enjoy small things: the sun, nature, a smile from others, the love of our children.

7. **To get rid of fear and worry, it helps to say goodbye to the past**. We must leave behind old thoughts and emotions. They hold us back from coming into our power and energy. Only when we let go of the past can a new future open up. You have the courage to leave old paths and take new ones—to be a pioneer and trailblazer. Tune into a new frequency—into a new lightness and joy.

8. **We should see life and everything around it as a whole**. Because everything is connected to everything. Therefore, we should say thank you today. We should say thank you for all the negative experiences in our lives. Because we wanted to experience these things. Now we have experienced them.
And so, the chapter is closed. A new chapter can begin—a new perspective, a new beginning—the start of a new world. Welcome! And we should say thank you for all the positive experiences our soul wanted to experience. What joy! What richness!

9. **Today, we may make peace—with ourselves, our parents, and our ancestors**. We may forgive them and reconcile with them. We carry many wounds within us—wounds that come from our family/ancestors and our childhood. We must understand that our parents and grandparents also suffered and carried these wounds. And whatever happened in our childhood: Our parents and grandparents also endured destinies. And we carry these within our system. They may now be healed.

10. **Today, we may come into trust**. The world and people are without trust. Have no fear. There is something greater that guides us. With our tiny minds, we cannot perceive the greater. But it is there. We are connected to something higher. And therefore, we may trust and have no fear. When we are in trust, we can let go. Only those who are afraid hold on and do not let go.

11. **The world now stands at a crossroads, and humanity must make a decision**. It has the freedom to choose one path or the other. One path is clinging to the old—money, the job, the material—and thus the fear of losing the old; and it is the struggle, the other battles of life.
Or one chooses the new world—without fear, without struggle, without holding on—simply living in the present and having trust in tomorrow—being in cheerfulness, lightness, and joy, and seeing the new world with the mind's eye. The old world leads to nothing. The new world leads to the rise of humanity and Earth, to healing and peace.

12. **The pursuit of 'always more' does not lead to cheerfulness and health**. We must no longer tie our happiness and joy to external things but seek and find them within ourselves. A different perspective on ourselves and our lives—our interactions with people, nature, and resources—changes us and the world. And that is what it is about: We all want to create a more beautiful world for ourselves, our children, and grandchildren. How do we get there? Something must first

happen within us. We must work on ourselves. Change begins within us: more heart, love, humanity.

13. **When we are cheerful and joyful, our relationships with perpetrators, enemies, and family are healed**. We then see them as friends and do joint projects with them that lead to joy. It is a cycle: When we are in joy, joy returns to us. And we can inspire others to rethink and embrace joy.

14. **Imagine a situation where you were incredibly happy**. Remember a situation, for example, as a child playing on the beach. The sun is shining, the waves are splashing. Other children are there. They have buckets, shovels, sieves, and other toys. You approach. You play together, build a castle, and use the toys.
In the evening, you go home with your parents. It was a beautiful, happy day. Did you want to take the toys with you? No! They were there to be used—for everyone! We do not need to flatter our ego through possession.

15. **Imagine a new situation where you were happy**—perhaps as a teenager or adult. You were in love. What did the feelings of happiness do to you? Did material things matter at that moment? Or your education, your job, your car, your own apartment? Were you happy? Why? Because of being in love or because of possessing material things?

16. **What do you need to be happy?** A car *(which is only there to be used, to get from A to B. It is not an object that makes a person happy—not even a Ferrari).*

What do you need to sleep well? I need peace! Do you need an apartment for that? Do you need a luxurious kitchen to prepare good and healthy food? I need people around me. Then I am happy.

Do I need a big apartment for that? No! I need beauty. And I find it by, for example, traveling by train and observing the landscape with lush green meadows, yellow flowers, mountains, lakes, and chatting with friendly fellow travelers.

17. **Do I need to own everything**: car, house, racehorse, motor/sailing yacht, vacation home to have joy? No! I cannot take these things with me when I leave the earth. I need some of these things for life. I need them to use, but also to own?

Am I happier if I own them? Perhaps "yes," because the feeling from childhood is there: only if I own things can I feel good. That is then a psychological problem!

18. **When we are cheerful and joyful, money also grows**. Because our previous negative actions with money are eliminated. And new money comes to us.

And then we use it for things that serve us (our heart) and the world, and not just generate a monetary profit but primarily an immaterial one: joy—joy in seeing the investment grow—whether in the field or in people.

19. We have heard: **When we are in joy, money also grows**.
Here is a picture: When we plant a tree, start a new project, find new love, etc., and we give lots of heart, love, and spirit to the root/soil, then the tree, plant, project, investment, money grows and blooms.
Because with our higher consciousness, everything we invest in grows. The return is holistic: not only material but also immaterial – joy of life, health, enthusiasm, lightness, purpose.

20. **What do money and lightness have to do with each other?**
Nothing! Only when we see money differently does lightness come into play. But we humans see money as "heavy." And it is cold. It does not feel warm. But when we laugh and rejoice, money rejoices too.
If we want to come into lightness, we should see money joyfully. Then it comes to us with ease and joy. Because we give money appreciation. Money wants to be "seen" and "noticed"— perceived as energy. Then it returns to us—many times over.

21. **The most important things in life: mental health and contentment**. Contentment is the prerequisite for mental and emotional (and spiritual) health.
When we are content within, we do not need to accumulate as much possession on the outside. How do we achieve contentment?

It is about the merging of inner and outer values
the inner and the outer
the material and the spiritual
the male and female energy
the individual and society
the left and right hemispheres of the brain.

Thus, balance (Yin/Yang) is achieved. And thus, equilibrium is created: in people and among people. Through merging, people come into a higher consciousness.
The result of our transformation and new perspective is: happiness, joy, purpose, contentment, and thus health.

22. **Conclusion: The source of health and healing lies within us**. We experience this source and thus happiness through self-awareness and focusing on our inner wealth instead of the outer. This new spirit and a healthy way of living lead to happiness.

When we integrate light (= highest frequency), love, and lightness into our lives, we create cheerfulness, inner contentment, and health.

23. **To achieve success for mental and spiritual health, a profound change in humanity's thinking is needed**. We must learn to live healthily, including:

- No striving for "more" (more consumption, more profit, higher salary, bigger car/house)
- No attachment to ego and material values
- No mobile phone (news) or other addictions
- No stress (in the family, at work, on the train/car)
- No bad diet (too much salt, sugar, fast food)
- Lots of physical activity in nature
- Lots of sleep
- Good, positive thoughts
- Meditation every day
- Constant smiling

24. **How did I come to cheerfulness and joy?** How did I find inner happiness? By letting go of ego, material things, and the pursuit of recognition and external success; by being grateful for what I have experienced; by forgiving; by meditating; by leading a healthy lifestyle, and so on.

There is no recipe. You have to experience and feel it.
"There is no road to happiness.
Because HAPPINESS is the road.

3. Chapter: Discover the Power Within You

You were born into this world to help us all rise to a higher level of consciousness. To do this, you need to find stillness and do the inner work. Right now, it's not so much about taking big steps outwardly, but about first going through the inner processes. This is about fully coming into your own power, independent of what is happening externally.

Free yourself from everything that still prevents you from being in your power.
- Where do you still have limitations?
- Where do you still hold beliefs that make you feel small?
- Where are there still people who drain your energy and prevent you from fully coming into your power?
- What behavioral patterns do you still hold onto that no longer serve you or bring you well-being (watching too much negative news, poor diet, unhealthy habits)?

Life is currently showing you clearly where you still need to move. The old ways no longer work. So, open yourself now to the new energy that wants to come into this world through you!

Your pure soul energy, your primal power—the energy that can transform everything—is within you. But you have closed the doors to it. Now is the time to open those doors again and truly return to your own power, no matter what happens externally, regardless of what others around you do or don't do. It's about you. It's about your journey. It's about your power. Have the courage to take new paths, perhaps paths that no one before you has walked, but that are ready to be walked now!

(Text by Henrike Pelaez)

The signs are increasingly pointing towards change. What do you no longer need in your life (maybe old thought patterns, negative emotions that need to be released, people who no longer serve you, life situations that need change), and what do you want to invite in (perhaps more joy, people with positive energy, new projects that help you and the world)? Take some time to reflect on this.

More than ever, a shift in mindset is needed. It's time to let go of old wounds and awaken to your authentic self. Ask yourself: Who am I really—who was I before the world (parents, society) began to "program" me, before I adapted myself to please my parents or society? What is my "authentic self"?

Every change starts within us. I invite you to step out of your comfort zone with me. Leave behind old thought- and emotional patterns. Most importantly, let go of your past—not the good parts, but those that hold you back from being in YOUR power, fully and authentically in YOUR energy. Only when we release the past can a completely new future open up to us, and we need this new future so urgently in this world. Stepping out of old (reaction) patterns into new ease and joy takes courage.

Courage to leave familiar paths and take new ones, to be a pioneer and a trailblazer. Align yourself with a new frequency, create new perspectives, and allow yourself to be more in your true power every day!

Together, we can leave the past behind and create a new future for us all. Everything always begins with the realization that we want to change something in life. Knowing what we want to let go of and what we want to invite instead. Therefore, take your time and calmly reflect on the questions above.

Then make a powerful inner intention to realign yourself. For example: "I intend to let go of my fears and limitations this year in order to activate my potential and experience newfound freedom. To do this, I want to surround myself with more positive people who inspire me and help me be in my power."

Now comes the most important part: the daily inner "work." Yes, you must do something every day to bring about positive changes. What you do depends largely on your intention. Since every change begins within, it is optimal to look inward: What can I do to stay in good energy? What helps me come into my power? There are countless possibilities: walks, singing mantras, meditating, fasting from news and media, attending seminars to get inspired, listening to healing music, laughing, dancing, singing…

I believe in a new world. I believe that right now is the right time to leave the old behind and finally return to our primal power. The more people have the courage to take this path, let go of old thought and emotional patterns, release the past, and discover who they really are and what still lies within them, the faster we will see positive change in this world.

(Text by Henrike Pelaez)

We all carry a beautiful soul frequency within us. But we have become so entangled in worldly matters that we have completely forgotten who we really are.

So much new light is currently coming into the world, bringing with it unimagined possibilities. It has never been easier to leave all limitations behind us. It is about coming into a new and actually ancient frequency. No longer making the old roles, stories, and concepts real, but courageously walking new paths. YOUR paths!!!

Question everything you hold to be true, because it may now lose its validity, and a new, higher truth may emerge! Become empty—only then can something new come. And then see what wants to come into the world through you out of that emptiness!

How many concepts, roles, and identifications do we carry with us that actually do not belong to us at all? At some point, we were told how we should be (to be loved by our parents or to fit into society or school) and how we should not be. We were silenced when we were "too outspoken," and we were told to "become something" (which threw us out of the pure feeling of "being enough"). My grandmother always insisted that I be well-behaved, diplomatic, and neat. But in my essence, I was wild, playful, and direct :) Which traits were suppressed in you?

Do you dare to really stand in your truth? Or are you afraid to show yourself? Do you even know what your truth is? Who you are and what makes you at your core?
What roles (as a woman/man, mother/father, employee, etc.) have you taken on that do not truly reflect your essence? Is everything we have learned and with which we identify really true? What is it that you truly want to bring into this world?

"If you do something you would do even without money, and it fulfills you, but you do it so well that others are willing to pay for it, then that is an indication that you have found your life's purpose!" Whatever that is—this answer lies within you alone—and you will only find it when you shed everything that is not you and enter the silence!

For a moment, let us forget all these roles, concepts, ideas, and identifications. All of this is not who we truly are. Let us shed layer by layer, wall by wall (we have built protective or heart walls due to many wounds), and discover who we truly are. Completely free. Completely authentic. Completely real. In this case, without regard for others. Because this kind of regard only continues to limit you.

When you find your true core, you will automatically have more love, more joy, more power, and more peace. For yourself and for those around you! But do not let yourself be held back any longer by people who vibrate differently from you, with whom you have to lower your energy or dim your light to be around. It is time to awaken. To remember your higher vibrations and to be authentically you once again. In this way, you will change your small world, and also the larger world.

The time for small steps is over. Have the courage to bring great things into the world. And the work always begins within: We break down our inner limitations and restrictions—this opens new (old) spaces within us, and automatically, when we are ready to let go of ego desires, the change that is needed for us, and for everyone else, can come into our lives! Have the courage to let go of your limitations and ego desires, and then see all that lies within you!

(Text by Henrike Pelaez)

"Courage is not the absence of fear, but the triumph over it."
Nelson Mandela

You alone have the power, the experience, the love, and the ability to master your life. The power is there. It rests within you, waiting for your awakening. Feel this power within you. Feel your heart and soul and let your power flow from you. Stop looking outside yourself. You are enough for yourself.

And within you, you will find everything you need. Trust in your own strength. In this way, you will find:
- Courage
- Serenity
- Compassion
- Patience
- Persuasiveness
- Willpower.

Trust that you can succeed. And open yourself to your shadows, not to eliminate them, but to lovingly acknowledge and gently master them. Transform your shadows into strength. You can transform them if you accept, respect, and lovingly embrace them. Only what we reject within can destroy us. What we love and accept as part of us will strengthen and protect us.

4. Chapter: The Challenges to Happiness

Everyone wants to experience the feeling of happiness, life satisfaction, joy, lightness, enthusiasm, humor, curiosity, creativity, spirituality, and wisdom.

Science tells us that humans are made up of 80% emotions. And they are not always positive. Negative feelings generally have a bad reputation. Anger can lead to crossing boundaries, jealousy can destroy relationships, and no one wants to be constantly surrounded by people who radiate sadness and heaviness. These challenging emotions often remain hidden because many people find it difficult to talk about them. Yet negative feelings can provide important clues about our needs.
We must learn to become aware of our feelings and gain control over them. Otherwise, they play roulette with us or dance the tango. And we must learn to talk about our feelings.

I couldn't talk about my feelings when I was a child, nor as a teenager. Only after I arrived in Latin America and lived there for a long time, experiencing how people naturally showed and expressed their emotions, did I open up. I, too, began to show my feelings.

Later, back in Hamburg, I became aware of my emotions toward my family. The suppressed emotions from my childhood and teenage years gradually resurfaced. Situations in the family and provocations emerged that triggered anger, aggression, resentment, and sadness in me. I was put down, not heard, excluded, underestimated - not sly, greedy, or immoral like my family.

Or I was angry with my colleagues or family because they lied to me. Thus, I could not be cheerful and happy before my time in Latin America, nor afterward. In Chapter 6, I am writing more about this topic.

But it wasn't only the family situation that sometimes hindered my happiness; work and life did too. I wasn't granted financial compensation for my outstanding performance at the bank. It was a battle lasting six months. I was irritable and aggressive, unable to sleep for nights.

Many people encounter issues throughout their lives that challenge their happiness. One of these obstacles is personal ambition. Ambition can already be at play during childhood and adolescence. It certainly takes its course during education and after entering the workforce. People want to achieve this or that—a higher position in the company, more salary, an apartment, a car, starting a family, more vacation.....
When wishes don't come true, some people become restless, annoyed, stressed. And then happiness cannot take center stage.

Another issue is frustration, which I myself have experienced many times. Why do we get frustrated? It is the unmet expectations that frustrate us—for example, my unmet expectations of business deals, acquiring new clients, unmet capital gains or profits, lack of success in love, and so on.

Conclusion: We need to separate ourselves from energies that do not do us good. We also need to question and rethink the beliefs we learned as children. Much of what we face as adults in terms of problems and challenges originates in our childhood—our upbringing, experiences, parents. This extends even to criminal behavior. A child who experiences domestic violence, sexual abuse, or other traumatic events at the hands of their parents may later act out in adulthood.
Psychological disorders in childhood need to be healed before they turn into perpetrators later in life. And we must start talking about these issues in school and take preventive measures. It is about rethinking and shifting perspectives. It's no longer about fighting symptoms but addressing the causes.

We must help young people today who—due to childhood traumas or experiences during their time in the womb—went through events that led them to anger, aggression, and hatred. We must prevent them from later resorting to weapons and taking their pain out on others. These people need psychological care. Their souls may want to experience taking another person's life. When young or not-so-young people pick up weapons and hurt others, something is wrong inside them. These emotional problems must be treated, and the root cause identified.

As previously written: Intervention must begin in early childhood, observing and making parents aware of these issues. Later, in school, teaching about family conflicts and their emotional consequences, as well as introducing preventive measures before violent outbreaks occur.

We must, therefore, pay more attention to early childhood development and care, so that children can navigate their later lives more successfully and not repeat the actions they experienced from their parents. The energy from our family home does not automatically leave us when we leave it. Energy travels with us. We must eventually separate ourselves from the destructive energies.
Mental health is, therefore, a highly sensitive topic—not just for adults but starting in childhood.

There are also other emotional issues faced by people who, as children, were not "seen" by their parents. They were cared for, but emotionally they were left alone by their parents: Who am I? What am I capable of? Who will help me be brave and confident? These children experience no violence and were not abused, but they carry subtle wounds within them, wounds that remain until the end of their lives. Because this deep-seated feeling of abandonment can continue. As a result, people may fall into hyperactivity, drinking, or other behaviors like gambling. We must face our traumas.
Emotional wounds are among the greatest challenges. And they do not make us happy.

We do not have to repeat the patterns that shaped our childhood and made us unhappy. We need to recognize and name our childhood wounds. Many people are preoccupied with the themes of "love, childhood, relationships": how we love, how we struggle in our relationships—all of this is connected to our childhood. Many relationship problems point to unresolved childhood issues. Even wounds like a father watching their child play sports and getting upset because they made mistakes. Some parents then label the child as worthless.

Children do not understand that adults have their own conflicts when they scold them. They do not recognize that the parents' anger is only partly about them—a fatal misunderstanding because from these wounds arise beliefs that we adopt without realizing it. For example:
  - I am not good enough.
  - I must be perfect to be loved.
  - I am only valuable if I achieve something.
  - I cannot trust anyone.

We must make peace—with ourselves and our family members. We carry many wounds within us—wounds that come from our family/ancestors and our childhood. We need to understand that our parents and grandparents also suffered and bore these wounds. And whatever happened in our childhood: our parents and grandparents also endured fates.
And we carry this into our system (into old age). They must be healed. We need to free ourselves from these wounds, like

emotional injuries of not being seen, being left alone, the emotional absence of mother/father, not being loved, etc.

There are many challenges that hinder people on the path to happiness and do not lead to that goal. When people argue, when they are angry and furious, when they are frustrated or envious, when they always want more and are never satisfied, and especially when they are fearful (and there are many different fears), they cannot be happy.

Being content with little makes one happy. It means no longer having the compulsion to want more, to buy, to consume. This also eliminates "frustration shopping," which many women like to do. Just pause—feel calm within yourself—enjoy the sunlight. That makes one happy.

> *"Whoever has found themselves once can lose nothing in this world anymore."*
> Stefan Zweig

Another example of a lack of deep happiness I see in Switzerland. Although the country is among the wealthiest in the world, and thus its citizens, in my eyes, they are not truly happy. There are several reasons for this. In any case, the origin of these reasons lies in the history of the country and thus in the families into which the current generation was born. This means that their parents and ancestors also did not experience and live deep happiness.

Since my background is in finance, I look at the topic particularly from this perspective. Money holds great importance among the Swiss. But people do not talk about money. It is kept silent. I believe that this is one of the reasons for hindering true happiness. Because on one hand, there is a focus on money. On the other hand, the money is not always clean. The doctors in psychiatric clinics have not yet addressed this money issue and its correlation with mental illnesses. I have pointed it out to some.

Switzerland has the largest offshore market for international funds. But these international funds were not all acquired legally. This did not interest the Swiss, especially the banks, lawyers, notaries, trustees. Only in the last 10-20 years has there been greater attention paid to the origin of the funds. But there are consultants who continue to obscure or cloud illegitimate funds through corporate, fund, or foundation structures.

The funds of the Russian tsars at the turn of the century, the funds of Persia in the 1930s, the funds of the Kurds, the funds of the Jews during World War II, as well as the funds of African and Latin American autocrats and Russian oligarchs—all ended up in Switzerland. We know that some of these funds are stained with blood. This has an impact on the country and the mood of the Swiss.

Then there are the many international organizations and companies—many of them based in Geneva or Zug. Here too, morally and ethically questionable business practices are used, generating money—money that is not clean. This weighs on the soul of Switzerland and its citizens.

And a third point is the appropriation of foreign funds by the Swiss. Some time ago, I heard a Swiss person on the street say to another, "Be glad that Hitler existed." At first, I couldn't make sense of this statement, but later I did. Some German Swiss sided with Hitler, others did not. But Hitler, or rather the war, filled some Swiss pockets—private individuals, companies, and institutions—gold refiners, i.e. Emil Bührle, etc.

The funds that Germans and other nationalities had entrusted to Swiss banks, insurance companies, lawyers, or trustees for safekeeping were only returned after the war if the descendants provided 100% proof. But the descendants could not provide this proof. The account holders had perished in concentration camps. And all correspondence (deposit and account statements, safe documents, etc.) with the bank had been withheld by the bank during the war for security reasons. The descendants, therefore, had no bank documents and thus no proof of their family's account in Switzerland.

Swiss banks, lawyers, and others have accumulated much guilt by making their clients' assets their own. Morality and ethics played no role. The respectable banks, insurance companies, lawyers, as well as the seed capital of some of the richest Swiss families, are stained with the blood and death of the original account holders.

The descendants of these Swiss carry the burden of their families. The high suicide rate among Swiss youth and their depression are partly due to the dishonorable acquisition of the original family wealth.

And not only psychological issues, but also the general reserve, discretion, and secrecy of the Swiss, in my eyes, trace back to the originally unethical acquisition of money. The introverted, non-open and transparent, mysterious nature of the German Swiss in particular has to do with Switzerland's past. It correlates with the safekeeping, management, and non-return of foreign funds.
People do not talk about money. They remain silent. Because there is something to hide. And this hiding leaves a mark on the soul. It is not free. It does not feel free. It is repressed—like many Swiss.

And this can still be felt in the present generation: tense, withdrawn, not relaxed. Of course, other factors also play a role. But the family home and the issue of money have a great influence. People have never learned to embrace each other. Children lack the loving hug—the felt love.

Whether there is a causal connection between the acquisition of unethical funds or the appropriation of clients' money and the lack of deep happiness among the Swiss could be a research project for a Swiss university or foundation. I brought this up to the Max Planck Institute in Munich years ago.

Today, values such as morality, ethics, and sustainability have entered the consciousness of more and more people and companies and are becoming part of the rules of the new era—worldwide. Perhaps it helps to transform "ethics and morality" into "ethics and spirituality" and to take a completely new path (instead of using power for personal gain) and grow beyond one's own "I", taking on the role of guardian of the planet. Because true power is about collective creation, not dominance, ego, and profit.

If this path is also taken in Switzerland, and if money is handled differently—for the benefit of people (see also Chapter 7)—then happiness and joy will soon emerge among the Swiss.

> *"New paths arise by walking them."*
> Friedrich Nietzsche

I have compassion especially for the younger generation—students, pupils, etc., not only in Switzerland but in many countries around the world. As I heard in my interviews with representatives of countries during the retreat in India, they are stressed and not truly happy. An English professor teaching at a university in Africa and recently invited to a lecture at ETH Zurich said I should bring happiness and humor to ETH. Because the lectures are very serious—as in many universities around the world, she said.

> *"Happiness is the joyful inner feeling of being in harmony with one's destiny."*

In my life, I have met various people who radiate happiness, such as Bojana. At a lakeside bathing facility in Zurich, an angelic being sits and enjoys the sunlight on her face. Her eyes are closed, and she smiles the entire time. I observe her and wonder what she thinks inside. In any case, I feel a total balance between her inner and outer self. I approached her and made contact. Later, we walk home together and share our life experiences. What a gift I received that afternoon.

Or the cashier at a supermarket chain. She is constantly smiling. What a joy to come to the supermarket and see this person's smile! And she has kind words for every customer. She greets everyone at her checkout warmly and lovingly. I asked her how she came to be like this. She said she had been cheerful, happy, and content since childhood. But I shouldn't think she hadn't suffered misfortunes. A lot, she said.
Among other things, as a child, she lied repeatedly. As punishment, her father made her kneel on rice grains for hours until she told the truth. The rice grains hurt incredibly. She swore never to lie again. How wonderful to see people so cheerful after misfortunes!

A friend told me about her first husband. He wanted her to stay home in front of the stove. They had no children. So, she wasn't allowed to work or pursue a career. He earned enough.
After eight years of marriage, he left her on the recommendation of his religious teacher. She had nothing. She was now 30 years old, had no money, no apartment, and no self-confidence

because her husband had kept her down. But something showed her the way to open her own bridal shop. She did so and gradually gain more and more confidence, eventually getting good jobs as an employee and generating good income.

Today, she would love to thank her first husband for holding her back, which gave her the courage to open a business that led her to self-confidence and earning her own money. She is very happy to have had that experience with her first husband. Without him, she would not be in the situation she is today. Without him, she would not have experienced the good in life. Quintessence: One may be angry, sad, etc., at first, but in the long run, it was an advantage. Good comes in bad clothing, she says today.

I, too, am grateful to my wife for separating from me 14 years ago so that I could be free to walk "my" path, which is different from her life and soul path. Children or souls born to couples who eventually part is meant to be conceived by that father and mother. They are meant to learn—from both. This has been my belief for many years. At the same time, these children should be embraced by both parents in their hearts, and their love for the children should always be expressed, for example, by lovingly holding them or saying loving words.

Today, many adult relationships fail because the inner dimension is not developed. When there is no authentic exchange regarding moods, feelings, longings, intuitions, sensations, doubts, fears, insights, or dreams, the relationship becomes impoverished. Busyness cannot fill the inner emptiness. The outer reality is consumed to excess. Where has the inner world, the inner experience, gone?

Yet a new trend is becoming apparent: the Inner Development Goals. More about this at a later time.

Another story concerns two young women who suffer from the aftereffects of the Corona vaccines in various forms: rheumatism (at 35 years old), artery problems, and organ damage. One of them had previously also had cancer. This is nothing special for many. But what is special and admirable is that both laugh! Both are cheerful and happy. Both have moved from their hometowns to a beautiful place on Lake Constance and are more than content with their lives—despite their illnesses and their awareness that they will not live long.

In Chapter 8, I am writing about another person who transformed their challenges into love and light and thus came to happiness.

5. Chapter: How Do We Reach Happiness?

Viktor Frankl and Friedrich Nietzsche have both pondered the question of MEANING. This question is significant, especially when a crisis (life crisis) arises. And today, we are living in turbulent times. Therefore, it makes sense to engage with the other side – the joyful side of life, including "How do I reach happiness?" and "How do I embrace the lightness of being?" which brings us joy, contentment, and a sense of happiness. Because worries and fears surround us every day.

Happiness is a feeling. And our thoughts influence our feelings. So, we must pay attention to and observe our thoughts. Negative thoughts will come, but we let them go. We focus on the positive, even if the negative thoughts are more numerous.
We focus on positive thoughts by, among other things, avoiding news, media, stress, addiction, ego, and instead enjoy the little things: the sun, nature, a smile from a fellow human being, the love of our children.

We can ask ourselves: **What am I happy about?** My answer, for example:
- Every morning, I wake up with joy.
- I am neither downhearted nor lack motivation.
- I enjoy the sunshine every day (even if it's not visible).
- I am healthy and disciplined.
- I have two happy children.
- I rejoice in my gifts, talents, and experiences.

- One of my gifts is to engage with people in a playful way.
- I am no longer stressed: no more chasing clients or meeting employer-set targets.
- I have detached from material things and have no desire for more.
- I had a beautiful house, a Mercedes, and much more.
- I do not worry about what tomorrow will bring or whether I need to move from my home. The right thing will come to me. I am relaxed and not stressed.
- I enjoy bringing sunshine to others every day.

This happiness fills me with immense gratitude.

So: How do I become happy, free from fear and worries?
- Joy, fun, lightness instead of dissatisfaction, worries, stress. *Our stumbling blocks: Ego, ambition, family patterns, trauma, fears.*
- Appreciation. Gratitude. Forgiveness (of ourselves, family, wrongdoers).
- Meaningful "doing" = creating. No perfectionism. Letting things flow.
- Nutrition, exercise, sports.
- A new approach to money. Letting go of material burdens.

Many people would like to carry this lightness within themselves and radiate joy. But something holds them back. These obstacles trace back to their childhood, as we learned in the previous chapter. Too many things happened that prevent them from freeing themselves from their current corset (mental prison).

They do not feel free to express their emotions. Their feelings are locked away because society dictates rules and goals for individuals. Parents have pointed this out to the child from an early age. Many beliefs and behavior patterns also originate from our childhood.

But what is the most beautiful thing for a child that makes it blossom emotionally? Playing – simply playing, letting creativity and emotions run free, without parents or supervisors restricting the child's play – neither in time nor in space. In play, the child finds and feels enthusiasm. With this, trust, joy, love, and gratitude grow.

We are allowed to be children again, to let our thoughts and feelings run free, to be guardians of the earth and gold, to play the clown and do what is fun. We are allowed to encourage others to follow us as clowns, to be playful, and to make people happy. In this way, we spread our happiness in a world that is so serious. After all, it is no longer about what we do in the "real" world. It is about being happy and joyful.

We are invited to connect with our inner child, which symbolizes purity and wonder. This step encourages us to rediscover our childlike innocence – a state before our perception was clouded by the complexities of life.
Today is about seeing the world with new eyes, like a child marveling at the mysteries of life, unburdened by prejudice and preconceptions.

But how can we return to this state of innocence when our mind is filled with knowledge, experiences, and realities? The key lies in learning to calm our mind and shedding the layers of accumulated facts, tasks, and societal expectations. In doing so, we open ourselves to a gentler, kinder, and more fulfilling life.

Let us allow the innocence of the child within us to guide our perceptions today. By doing so, we pave the way for a journey full of surprises, joy, and the boundless potential to see the world anew – with fresh eyes.

However, soon we will be confronted with everyday life again. It shows us the negative sides of life once more, including traumas, entanglements, etc. These are stored in our subconscious. To travel the journey from child to adult and back to child with ease, it is necessary to work through and resolve the negative aspects within us. These hinder our happiness. To do this, we need to engage with our subconscious.

Our subconscious is particularly programmed with emotions and memories between conception and the age of seven. From birth, we divide the world into good and bad experiences. The subconscious stores this division, and later it appears to the conscious mind as real.

As we know, the subconscious is 1,000 times more powerful than the conscious mind. If the subconscious is so powerful, who or what controls it?

The source of everything that plagues us is our locked-away emotions, the injuries, fears, and unprocessed experiences that we hold captive in our nervous system. Behind every stress, symptom, or disease pattern—whether psychological or physical—are emotions and memories buried in our subconscious. When they are triggered, our body responds with negative stress.

We can trigger a stress reaction through thoughts alone. It is enough to think about something deeply etched within us. And immediately, memories of earlier situations come to life, becoming acute and real in that moment. Our brain functions in images. Thus, a thought arises within us that triggers an emotion. As a result, our heart rate increases, and we become anxious.

The core of every stress and illness is feelings and memories—traumatic perceptions buried in our subconscious. We must understand that our emotions and the human body are energy.

Our thoughts create our feelings, and our feelings control our behavior. When one of our emotions is very strong, we are actually feeling vibrational energy. Every feeling vibrates with its own specific frequency. Anger is different from frustration or sadness. All these feelings have different vibrational energies. With intense emotion, our entire being can be captured by that vibration. Sometimes, the vibration is too strong, and the energy remains trapped in the body. A trapped emotion is like an energy ball, which can lodge anywhere in the body and disrupt the normal energy field.

In ancient times, people knew that negative feelings are stored throughout the body. They affect the body's emotional and anatomical functions. Feelings become dense, and the stronger they get, the more we push them away. We were taught to resist unpleasant feelings rather than allow and feel them. We look for answers in the external world, but the problem is that we find nothing there. The answers are within us, as are the feelings. Only when we look inward can we experience ONENESS—a connectedness with all things, including the universe.

We know the power of the mind. It is scientifically proven that it can heal itself—over and over again. The universe supports us when we participate and believe. Together with the universe, we can create something. The universe always has a solution for us. Do not ask for what you want, but simply give thanks. When you ask, it implies that you do not have it. When you give thanks, you acknowledge that it is already there.

When we release the chains of emotional dependence, true transformation occurs. The side effect of this true transformation is called JOY. This elevated state of mind occurs when energy is freed from the body. The body is released from the past and arrives in the present. Then we feel the other kind of feelings: joy, goodwill, and gratitude.

When we allow ourselves to feel and be fully present, everything becomes possible. The world around us becomes very malleable, moldable, and magnificent.

Here are some messages:

Everything is ENERGY. Everything is consciousness.

Feelings are the energy that drives you. This inner life force enables you to be who you truly are. Transform what you do not want into what you desire.

We may "observe" the dramas and traumas of life, but not become entangled in them. Just observe.

We may shed our beliefs and dive into our true, heart-centered power.

We may overcome fear. We may enter a state of fearlessness in which our actions are guided by love. Love—deep, unconditional love—is the strongest force against fear.
Love is my shield, transforming fear into strength.

The luminous warrior does not seek division but deep healing, recognizing that the root of conflict often lies in our own shadow. At the heart of the luminous warrior's path is the transformation of fear into love. Fear, seen as the absence of love, is transformed through forgiveness and gratitude. Forgiving those who have hurt us and feeling grateful for the lessons they brought us is the first step toward empowerment and healing. This process allows us to recognize that the challenges of life do not happen to us but for us, offering opportunities for growth and deepening our humanity.

If we take this path, we let go of the need to be right by making others wrong, and instead cultivate a presence filled with love and compassion. Through forgiveness and gratitude, we transform our toxic emotions into personal power and step into the role of the luminous warrior, who creates beauty in the world and recognizes that everything in life (even the most challenging experiences) ultimately contributes to our growth.

I master my fears with the courage and light of the luminous warrior. Love is my greatest weapon. It transforms fear into opportunities for growth.

One of the collective traumas is the excessive masculine approach, which often marginalizes the feminine. This must be acknowledged and healed.
We need to engage with the historical oppression of the feminine. Especially in Western traditions, there has been an attempt to domesticate the feminine and suppress its inherent wildness and freedom. This oppression manifests itself in societal structures and personal interactions, often in ways that restrict and confine the feminine spirit.

The concept of hysteria reflects deep-seated fears and misconceptions about feminine power. It has led to practices aimed at removing the wild, untamed aspects of femininity, thereby creating a controlled femininity.

The re-emergence of the Wild Woman is crucial not only for societal roles but also for each individual. It's about liberating the inner feminine and allowing it to express itself fully, without being constrained by conventional limits. It challenges the fear of change and uncertainty by embracing innovation and the unknown.

I release the past and embrace renewal.

I let go of what no longer serves me, making space for new beginnings.

We are called to question our belief systems, the ones we navigate life with, to discern which serve us and which we must let go. This self-reflection frees us from negative energies, enabling growth and the emergence of new beginnings and potential. This energy rises through the chakras of our body, symbolizing transformation and enlightenment.

I release what binds me and find strength and liberation in my upward journey.

I recognize and transform my inner shadows into light and love. Our deepest wounds require our urgent attention. It's about profound inner healing. And this leads to happiness.

We need to identify and heal toxic, traumatic attachments and not inflict pain on ourselves.

Every moment is an opportunity to rewrite my story.

I am centered and at peace—independent of the storms around me.

I observe the events of my life from a distance, gaining clarity and wisdom.

When you do something that makes someone else feel better, you too feel better.

I am whole, and every part of me is welcomed and loved.

I accept my whole self with compassion and understanding.

I am a channel for healing—for myself, for others, and for the Earth.

The wisdom of the past lights my way forward.

Guidance and insight flow easily to me when I connect with my heart.

I trust my journey through life and see each crossroads as an opportunity for growth.

I am surrounded by love and radiate this love outward. Self-love is the foundation of my strength and the source of my connection to others.

I meet the world with joy and lightness.

Every one of my actions contributes to the healing and well-being of the planet.

As a guardian of the Earth, I am connected to the web of life, nurturing the Earth and being nurtured by it.

By practicing stillness, we learn to influence our reality in its most malleable state before it solidifies into form. This approach mirrors the teachings of many Native American societies, reminding us that our actions and thoughts have an impact over seven generations.

Today, we are called to dream with open eyes and imagine the changes we wish to see, implementing them from a place of deep inner stillness. It is a call to attentively consider the impact of our thoughts and actions and choose those that foster a world we desire for ourselves and future generations.

We are allowed to dream a new world—a future of harmony, responsibility, and peace.

> *"Never give up on a dream just because it takes time to achieve it. Time will pass anyway."*
> Earl Nightingale

The source of health and healing lies within us. We experience this source, and thus happiness, through self-awareness and by focusing on our inner wealth rather than the external. This new spirit, along with a healthy way of living, leads to happiness.
By integrating light (= highest frequency), love, and ease into our lives, we create joy, inner contentment, and health.

We wish to bring people into serenity, cheerfulness, light-heartedness, and joy. How do we achieve serenity and joy? By letting go of ego, materialism, and the pursuit of recognition and external success; through gratitude for what we have experienced, through forgiveness, through meditation, and through a healthy lifestyle, etc. To be content and thus happy with little. And then comes confidence and joy.

1. By not identifying: Who am I? Where do I come from?
Many people are still caught up in their ego and have not understood what it is about on a soul level—namely, understanding that it is not about success, recognition, and money but rather:
- that we are allowed to learn a higher understanding and insight,
- that success and recognition have nothing to do with the external (the material) but that we are allowed to seek and find it WITHIN ourselves.

Our true happiness comes from within and not because of our external possessions.

2. We live in a world where we must leave behind the old, where we are allowed to rethink and transform. NEW awaits, ready to be tackled.

The old includes our conception of life: education, job, earning money, marriage, children, illnesses, job loss, fears of financial decline, sadness, loneliness, possible depression, loss of social status, aging, and death.

3. Instead, I allow positive energy to flow into me every day.

4. Additionally, I dissolve the blockages within me (created by myself, my family, and society). And I change my beliefs.

5. A person's capital is not money.

Capital is potential, talents, courage, creativity, cheerfulness, health, etc. And capital also includes morality, honesty, transparency, and trust. With this capital, one can always create something new.

6. However, when it comes to fate, we are allowed to look at it. But we should not see ourselves as victims. Instead, our soul wishes to experience this fate. We are allowed to grow from it: accept it with calmness and understanding, and approach it with ease (not heaviness).

7. What are the handicaps to becoming happy?
- Childhood injuries and traumas
- Conditioning from parents and society
- Psychological pressure from oneself or from outside

- Lack of acceptance of a culture of failure
- Stress about earning money, but also seeing money as a
  burden
- Doubts about oneself and one's abilities
- No role models as parents, politicians, business leaders
- Fear of failure.

How do we find contentment and lightness?
- A new perspective on life, work, money, consumption, etc.
- Mentally stepping out of the system (not feeling trapped anymore)
- No fear of failure—in front of society, parents, friends, partners
- Not taking oneself too seriously
- Less perfectionism (stress), ego, addiction to "more"
- Less focus on material values
- Less conformity, envy, jealousy, etc.
- Not seeking recognition through money (from parents, partners, friends)
- Healing family issues. The cause of many things lies in our childhood or home: relationships, money, emotional issues, soul wounds, depression, etc.
- More into heart power, intuition, feeling
- Making peace with perpetrators, enemies, etc.
- Opening the heart and soul (= spirit)

Thus, lightness, intuition, inspiration, creativity, etc.

8. How do I earn money?

We humans see money as "heavy." And it is cold. It does not feel warm. But when we laugh and rejoice, money rejoices too. Then it comes to us with ease and joy. Because we give value to money.

When we are satisfied inside, we don't need to accumulate as many possessions outside. And then we can use money for other things, e.g., helping other people find joy or independence, etc.

We need to find joy, ease, and light-heartedness within ourselves, not externally.

Make peace with others. Forgive perpetrators/enemies. Reconcile.
Be grateful for your life, your family, your children.
Tell your loved ones how grateful you are for everything.
When you smile at people, a smile comes back.
Radiate joy.
Show helpfulness. Work on your own inner wars. Take time for yourself and others. Surround yourself with happy people instead of pessimists, critics.

"Remember that happiness is not a goal but a journey,
and it's okay to have ups and downs along the way.
Be patient with yourself and continue striving
to create a life that brings you joy and fulfillment."

6. Chapter: My Journey to Happiness

Happiness is perceived differently by everyone, and it reaches deep into the psyche. It has roots in childhood. Was my home a happy one—my parents, grandparents, my siblings, and me? Or was my childhood dominated by competition, survival, financial struggles, or other challenges? Why was I happy back then, or why not?

About myself: I was not a happy child or teenager. As the firstborn to parents striving for prosperity in post-war Germany, dedicating their time to work and earning money, and giving little to their children, I grew up in the 1950s and 1960s. I was completely introverted, sad, struggled in school, and skipped classes often. I attended five schools in total and finished without a degree. It wasn't until I trained as a banker and left my family—moving abroad for work—that I slowly found my path.

My career as a banker went fantastically. I was cheerful. I laughed. I was successful. I felt like the master of the universe. Yet, I was somewhat arrogant, not truly in touch with my heart, and far from my soul's desire. And thus came the obstacles—the challenges. I was shaken awake. I was in my ego, immersed in materialism—like everyone else. My goal was to earn a lot of money. That was, and still is, a set goal for many people. But, as I later learned, it wasn't supposed to be my goal. I had to face bankruptcy. I had to leave my beloved city of Miami.

Before that, I had to sell our wonderful house. In Hamburg, I had to scale down—no more luxury, no rich people or "friends" around me, no more high-society cocktails—just living like many others.

So, I went through tough times for the next seven years. In Hamburg, I easily found a position at UBS – the Swiss Bank. But after three months, I was effortlessly dismissed, as they realized I had just turned 50, and under German law, it's harder to dismiss someone over 50. So, they did it during my probation period.

After this personal setback, I managed my small fortune and turned it into a large one—a very large one. But fate had other plans. For three years, I experienced the same cycle: my investment tripled at first; I held onto it for a long time, and then it crashed. I took another amount and invested again. Once more, it tripled, I held onto it, and it crashed. I did it a third time— my last bit of money. Again, it tripled. This time, I held my gold and silver investments for only a short time before it all dissolved through margin calls.

An incredible experience in those three years. Around the same time, my brother, a well-known medical doctor, took his own life. I had no intention of following him. Through him, I came to alternative medicine and later to spirituality. I spent many years on this subject, growing internally.

In 2015, I was introduced to a psychic medium. She told me that I would make people happy. "You are a happiness-maker," she said. I was surprised. As a child and teenager, I was totally introverted, sad, and reserved. I became happy abroad but grew arrogant and materialistic. Then I got a setback in the form of bankruptcy and later financial loss. Afterward, I searched for years for "my" path, the one my soul desired.

And now I was informed by the psychic medium that I am a happy person and will make others happy because they are not. "Do not think it is normal for everyone to be happy and joyful. No, it is not a given. It's a gift, and you have received it. That's why it is normal for you. And because people don't have this gift, they are interested in being close to you. They feel comfortable around you and laugh with you." I have indeed often experienced this.

She continued, "You are undergoing a major transformation, like a caterpillar becoming a butterfly - a profound process. You too will go through this enormous process - from aggression, anger, resentment, and frustration that you have carried with you all your life, to joy, happiness, transformation, and becoming a diamond.

Bit by bit, you free yourself from influences that caused anger, irritation, self-doubt, resistance, hurt, grief, and sadness. It's about cutting all ties from your past experiences to become free. There will no longer be any attachments leading to frustration, impatience, or accumulation of possessions. You will be free from these attachments and energies.

You will be able to fully detach from and liberate yourself from these emotional influences. This, in turn, gives you a higher state of consciousness and a broader perspective through which you can see the world and your place in it. Perhaps the greatest part of this transformation is how you see yourself in the world.

It's about a whole new dimension. It's practically like a soul journey – you migrate (or transform) out of emotional forms into freedom and deeply into yourself. Through this transformation, you feel much better about what you do and how you do it. You let go of your serious, ambitious, and perfectionist nature. You become cheerful, playful, childlike.

And you bring people the fruits of life – unconditional joy in living. What is the essence of life? The essence is to enjoy – enjoy being alive, having the privilege of being here on Earth. Our birthright is to lead a deep, meaningful, purpose-driven life in joy.
You will bring people to joy and contemplation through your joy and laughter, prompting them to change their perspectives on life. It's about celebrating life and embracing it with joy.

Life is immense. The more we embrace true life, the happier we become. The more we dive into life, the more fun it brings us. And the more interesting life becomes. We become humble. It is much deeper than many people realize. We just need to be ourselves - not what we should be or want to be or would like to be – just be ourselves. 'I am funny; I am silly; I love to joke; I love to have fun; I love to play; I love to have sex.'

Everything others have told me I should do, or what my ego said to do to achieve something, I no longer care about. I just want to be happy. I no longer judge. It is what it is. Let it be. It is an honor for me to share things with you that bring me joy." And then they find joy in it. You simply spread joy and laughter! And they share it with others.

Life is laughter. It is fun. You make jokes. It is nothing serious. At the same time, it is much more serious than anyone can ever imagine. It is joyful. And people want this joy in a world where there is so much distress, misery, and suffering that it becomes unbearable for many. You bring what the doctor ordered: lightness, cheerfulness, and happiness.
You enrich them. Everyone laughs. When they go home, they feel free and full of hope. They feel rescued – from sadness, depression, and worries. Because you convey wisdom to them in a way that speaks to their inner child.

And in doing so, you remove judgment and separation from consciousness. We all have this paradigm of separation: "This part of me is good; the other part is not." That is judgment. And that is separation.
You show people both sides: the ability to laugh. And through your joy and laughter, you remove any notion of judgment.

People will experience your joy as the most wonderful, magical, nourishing, sustainable, and supportive input they have ever had. You give them the essence and the feeling of being reborn as their own child of God.

And you give "talks" in a light, playful, almost comedic way, which draws people's attention. When they leave, they smile. And they laugh. They go home and start thinking about your playful words. Because they are much more than just funny and amusing. They are profound wisdom presented in a light, childlike form.

Wow - I was really impressed. What a beautiful, enlightening, and motivating message. "The only thing that will not change – you are a healer. But how you heal will change. It is a healing through laughter, joy, and bringing happiness and sunshine."

And that I had to learn – to let my emotions run free: enthusiasm, joy, trust, love, gratitude. And to let go of all my anger, resentment, frustration. My soul apparently wanted me to eliminate these negative emotions in this life, to free myself from them.

But it did not happen overnight. It took me several years. Between 2016 and 2021, I was often in positive emotions but was repeatedly triggered by my family, which brought me back to anger, frustration, and resentment. Only when I drew a line and physically separated myself from my family by moving to Switzerland did I feel liberated. There, I could practice and live my freedom – my lightness, my joy.

Isn't it remarkable that in 2015 I received a message from someone, and eight years later I found myself physically in the country they had foreseen? With all the messages, she said: "You will go to Switzerland, and especially in southern Switzerland and northern Italy, you will find people who greatly appreciate your gifts and support you in your mission."

Secondly: Isn't it remarkable that I had to go through a difficult process from caterpillar to butterfly, from 2016 to 2021, reliving all my anger and resentment, especially towards my family, to then let go of my negative emotions?

The last negative emotions arose during my visit to Hamburg in June 2024. I recorded my resentment, anger, and frustration in the form of notes and sent them to my family. What was it about? I was never heard. I was never accepted, partly because of my lifestyle, which did not fit into the box of what an adult (according to my family) should be. According to their ideas, one should go to work, earn money, have an apartment, a car, perhaps a family, occasionally take a vacation, etc.
This was the life I had before. Now my life and lifestyle were different: less baggage but cheerful, laughing, almost childlike, playful, seeing the world with fresh eyes – unlike the box-thinking adults. I was an artist of life, filled with incredible joy.

My thoughts and opinions did not matter to my family. Only their opinions, conclusions, and judgments mattered – along with their egos and self-satisfaction.

But I have long since ceased to be disappointed and have forgiven them. Their souls wanted this experience, and so did mine. Their learning task will come to their consciousness at some point, perhaps triggered by misfortune. Many people change their thinking only after misfortune. And then cheerfulness, lightness, and laughter may enter our lives. We also realize that deep happiness settles within us when we are connected with universal energy.

Thirdly: Isn't it remarkable that I am now writing a book about happiness, a subject – an emotion that I carry within me?

> *"Where it leads, where you didn't want to go at all*
> *that is precisely where transformation happens."*

I received a similar message about my path to happiness in January 2024. Isn't it remarkable that two different people on two different continents and at two widely separated times gave the same message? The message in January 2024 was:

"You make people happy by bringing them joy. You make them aware that their attachment to their ego and material things brings neither joy nor bliss.
You tell them that you once had a lot of material wealth and then lost everything. When you had a lot, you were happy. But was that true happiness? Because when you had nothing, you were truly happy – from within (not from the outside). You lead people into meditation to reflect on themselves and their lives.

Some will understand - not all, but some. The stress level people are exposed to -worries, fears, and hyperactivity: constantly checking their phones, taking care of children, managing households, working, caring about appearance, accepting invitations, planning vacations, etc. – is very high. Added to this are worries about jobs, family, earning money, investing, etc. The body has to endure this stress level, which wears it down immensely and brings processes into turmoil.

It is about **detachment**: detachment from attachment to the ego and material exterior. It is about a shift in perspective. **People tie their happiness to their material wealth**.

I received a metaphor from the psychic medium: I am the last survivor of a concentration camp. Like some other prisoners, I always knew and felt that there was an inner source from which I could draw love, joy, and strength that kept me alive.

Just as the prisoners had nothing left after losing their material wealth, I too had nothing but access to a source that gave me hope, confidence, and joy every day. This joy I want to share with others.

I do nothing concrete - in the sense of the worker bees, i.e., society. I simply make people aware of their lives and share my own – which was as successful and materialistic as theirs – and how it changed afterward. I simply direct attention so that people recognize themselves – discover their joy. I do not have to transform. It transforms itself. Something starts to flow. It is abundance. It is wealth. I make the blind see.

Today we can discover what brings us joy. Happiness is about detaching from material possessions. "You may ask yourself: To what – to which things (objects/possessions) – everything in the 'have' domain – do you tie your sense of well-being and comfort? Would you feel better and happier if you had more - more money, more recognition, more possessions? Think about it. Take a deep breath. Feel inside. How wonderful is the inner light – the essence of your being. That is the source."

It is about feeling today that something deep is within me. There is a life in me that is happy in itself. It is about making the blind see and **activating their heart power. Joy has its home in the heart**. It cannot be felt anywhere else. And the heart is always close to the source - the source of life.

When I make a funny remark, it goes through the mind. But the heart laughs with it. What truly laughs is the heart. And that has a healing power—a calming energy. The body comes to rest. And when the body is at rest, everything regulates itself. The interesting thing is: Inflamed body cells then transform into neutrality and do not break out as disease.

Joy has the greatest transformative power that heals everything. Feeling joy heals everything. When you are in the light of joy, you automatically help people align themselves with joy. And out of joy, the world reshapes itself. New systems emerge from this. Through each individual who follows joy, something changes in the entire system. You do not need to apply a lever to change or get something moving. No, it realigns itself - from a different awareness. IT realigns, not I, not you, not he, she, or it. IT realigns.

In the energy of joy, everything comes together - everything necessary to bloom, to be fully present in one's nature, and to do good for the greater whole. In this energy, everything culminates. It is as if there were a super pill for all diseases.

"Life is lived forward and understood backward."
Søren Kierkegaard

How did I find inner happiness?
Through a shift in perspective regarding my views and beliefs about life. We are merely guests here on Earth. Therefore, we may practice serenity and not take things so seriously. We may question our separateness – man and woman, black and white, Jew, Christian, or Muslim – as well as our judgments.
We may question our consumerism. We may question our materialistic mindset. We may regain simplicity – being satisfied with little. We may transcend and dissolve our little or big "I," letting go of our ego.

How did I find inner happiness?
By letting go of the ego, material things, and the pursuit of recognition and external success; through gratitude for what I experienced; through forgiveness; through meditation; through a healthy lifestyle, etc. Thus, I experienced peace of soul.

Was I happy before? Yes, because of my success and my external wealth. Was I happier afterward? Yes! Because I found access to the source – to power, love, joy of life.

I live joy, laughter, and humor. I am a clown – the child of God. And with that, I make people laugh, bring lightness, and spread sunshine.

I feel like a child. At the end of the retreat in India, I had the input - the inner image: I saw myself as a 7-year-old child: laughing, playing, carefree, full of joy, curious, brave, creative, playing clown, making others happy (getting them out of their dull daily routine), having fun, being funny - without fear or worries.
I can also be serious. On the one hand, I have 70 years of life experience. On the other hand, I go back to childhood. I embody both sides: the experienced and the childlike. What a gift!

Life is a great enrichment. We are so fortunate to be here on this Earth. Life is so simple. We just need to learn the "game of life"— be cheerful, happy, dance, and bring joy into the world. And unite this joy with spirit. Because it is not about superficial joy, but about "joy beyond."

7. Chapter: Happy Money

Life and money are connected: without money, there is no life. And without life, there is no money. But is our life happy? And is our money happy?

Money carries immense weight in today's world. Our discomfort is indirectly tied to it. This is because we've focused on the external - the material - and neglected or pushed aside our inner selves. Thus, true happiness cannot arise.

First, the question: What exactly is money? ChatGPT answers: "Money is a universal medium of exchange used to measure, store, and trade the value of goods and services. It fulfills several core functions in the economy:

1. **Medium of Exchange**: Money facilitates trade by representing a general value, eliminating the need for direct barter of goods or services.

2. **Store of Value**: Money preserves purchasing power over time, allowing it to be saved and spent later.

3. **Unit of Account**: It allows for the valuation and pricing of goods and services, providing a common basis for comparing values.

4. **Means of Debt Settlement**: It is used to repay debts or fulfill financial obligations.

Money can exist in different forms: physically, as coins and banknotes, or digitally, as balances in bank accounts.
The acceptance of money is based on **people's trust in its value** and its ability to function as a medium of exchange and store of value."

Now to the question: **Can we still trust our monetary system?** But more importantly: **Can we be happy given our current awareness of money**? Does it bring us joy, ease, and lightness? Or does our current money mindset belong to the past? Does something need to change within us for us to be happy with money? These are all psychological or philosophical questions. The wealthy might say: We are happy. The poor might say: We are not.

There are 10% who are rich and 90% who are not. But from this, one cannot conclude that 90% are unhappy. Many of them are - internally. And many of the wealthy are not. Not all rich people are happy - outwardly, they appear to be, but inwardly, they are not. Their children in particular are searching for their purpose – their true "self."

So, I am concerned with the inner self, not the outer self. Many people seek happiness and bliss in external things, such as money, possessions, and accumulation. But happiness does not reside in the external; it resides within us.

For 40 years, I worked in the financial industry – initially in lending in Venezuela, and then for 25 years as a private banker for high-net-worth individuals in Latin America, the United States, and Germany. On the lending side, I provided substantial loans to large companies and government agencies. I saw how they handled the money. At the time, Venezuela was one of the wealthiest countries due to its oil. They didn't really need loans, but they used them to build various industries, which eventually collapsed - and with them, the money vanished as well.

As a private banker, I was responsible for acquiring new clients and managing their funds. I experienced firsthand how these people dealt with money. They were all entrepreneurs. Almost all of them started from scratch and had amassed wealth in the double- or triple-digit millions. I wondered how they had achieved this. Perhaps morality and ethics didn't play a significant role, as is still the case in today's business world. Driven by the pursuit of profit and competitive pressure, consumers are sold products - through clever, sometimes aggressive marketing - that appear to "shine" outwardly but are rotten inside. Customers feel happier with this product than with another, but in reality, they are merely dazzled by excellent marketing - that is, the promises made by the producer or service provider. Today's social media, like Apple, Google, Facebook, Instagram, WhatsApp, Telegram, TikTok, and Platform X, are helpful in this regard.
Social media, by the way, negatively impacts satisfaction and happiness.

In any case, I was my wealthy clients' doctor, therapist, and psychologist. In our personal conversations, we discussed their psyche, their feelings about their business, and their families. While the question of where to invest the money was only marginally addressed in our in-depth conversations, money nevertheless indirectly dominated the discussions.

Many of them wondered whom in their families they should entrust their wealth to and whom they should appoint as the successor to their business. Or how to protect their wealth: "How do I avoid losing what I have?" Fear thus plays a significant role here. Fear, along with greed, are the two drivers in finance.

I met and advised people with a great deal of money and observed their attitudes towards wealth. Many of them were focused on: How do I make more money from this? How do I earn even more (even though they already had 50 million or more)?

For others, 50 million was enough. They did something good with their money, such as investing in education and promoting young people. In other words, they handled money wisely and socially.

Yet others treated money recklessly – they won and lost. Either they had good instincts (gut-feelings), or they didn't.

On the other hand, in Latin America, I met people who had nothing – yet smiled from their hearts. In Europe, too, I encountered people with modest incomes who had their worries, but also an inner assurance that they would always be provided for.

It all depends on our **inner attitude**, whether we are happy or not - with a lot of money or with a little.

Many people, however, do not live within themselves but in the external world. They worry about money. They can't sleep, are workaholics, or drink, gamble, etc. (mostly wealthy people). They've lost the ground beneath their feet. Many clinics in Switzerland are filled with patients with these symptoms. The causes can be childhood or later traumas or beliefs - and money often plays a role. I've learned this from my own family of origin. However, this issue has not yet been fully addressed in clinics.

The dogma of money - whether rich or poor - is generally associated with worries, fear of loss, and greed. As a consequence, money is hoarded, leading to a blockage. The flow wants to move. Water must flow, and money should as well. But it no longer flows. Why not? **We have not dealt well with money**.

Moreover, family views on money are often shaped by a negative perspective. As previously mentioned, family backgrounds concerning money are a crucial factor. In our childhood, we heard many things about money from our parents and grandparents. These statements, opinions, and views about money were implanted in us. Perhaps we even absorbed them at conception or during pregnancy.

Furthermore, history has shown that money was often acquired unethically and immorally. Many families, at some point in their history, accumulated wealth in this way. There is much evidence of this. It's not only known to the Max Planck Institute but also to historians. I experienced this in my own family.

When we acquire wealth unethically, it has subconscious effects on the psyche, relationships, and finances within the family, lasting over generations.

What must happen for everyone to be happy with their money? We need to change our awareness. Money is an exchange medium, as we know. We need to handle this medium differently from now on - with love, joy, and kindness. We can give money to others - with love and from our hearts - whether to the cashier at the supermarket, the gas station attendant, or the waiter, wishing them all the best. We can honor money, love it, acknowledge it. This makes money "warm." So far, it's been "cold and emotionless." We can reverse the energy - imbue it with our feelings, because money is energy.

For many people, this is new. To them, money is dark, heavy, perhaps even black. Although money is neutral, people perceive it in various forms. It is we who have given money negative energy, or at least view it that way. But we have the power to change it. We have power over money. We can use it positively or negatively.

We can decide today which direction we and money will take. We can choose to see the energy of money differently. We can choose to love it, honor it, acknowledge it, and use it wisely.
If we treat money well and use it well, **it will bring joy and health** (rather than fears, worries, bad conscience, depression). This is the known principle of cause and effect.

We can now use our energy positively if we want to be happy, and if we want money to flow towards us. So far, we haven't treated money well. That's why it doesn't flow. Many people and many companies (VW, Mercedes, and many others) are already experiencing this. Money/profits don't flow like it used to. And soon, some governments or countries (USA, France, Italy) will experience it too.

To achieve happiness, we need a new, positive relationship with money. Only then can we find joy and happiness. And thus, we create HAPPY MONEY. We can imbue money with positivity. We can make money HAPPY.

Happy Money is not a new currency, but a new consciousness – a new perception of money. We need to change people's awareness. Our previous awareness lacked depth. It was tied to the era we lived in, aligned with historical circumstances. Initially, it was about survival. Money was used to save lives. We still see this today with people from Africa or crisis regions like Syria and Afghanistan, who pay smugglers to escape danger and reach a safe country.

During wartime, we Germans used money to buy food, to survive. Today, we use money to make more money, to multiply it. And many strive for more and more. As long as this striving doesn't serve the ego—to fill an inner void or to gain status—but serves the common good, it is acceptable.

Yet people in developing countries still struggle to survive. Money does not come easily to them. It feels heavy.

Today we live in a new era. Our view of life and money is changing. Many people are no longer satisfied with the old perspective. They feel stuck, drained, exhausted, lifeless. They are searching for something new—something that provides stability, hope, and joy. They are searching for a golden "ground" or a saving tree in the ocean.

Our task is to make money flow, to see money joyfully, to view money as "gold" and to transform our previously heavy and dark perception of money into a flow of Happy Money.

We need to share **this new and expanded awareness of money** with everyone—those in developing countries whose money flow is sparse, those in developed countries whose flow is steadier but still insufficient, and those whose income is already prosperous.

We need to leave behind our collective past and erase it from memory. **We have reached a higher level of awareness**, and with it, a new attitude toward money.

Some people will not immediately jump onto the happy money train. They still need to go through the experience of a limited money flow—as a learning task. But they will not suffer. They will not have to fight for survival. It is a lesson in making do with little. This also applies to people who previously had a lot and lived in abundance. They, too, will learn to be happy with less. Because, as we have always known: money does not bring happiness.

But we want to be happy. Because we have not treated money well and have focused more on the material rather than our inner selves, we are not happy. To become happy, we need to treat money differently and see it differently. Money wants to be happy. Through a different approach and perspective, it becomes happy. And then it comes to us.

When we focus more on **inner values** rather than material values, **Happy Money** emerges. And then we are happy. We become more interested in contentment, joy, and happiness rather than financial returns.
Money no longer runs smoothly, meaning the pursuit of financial returns is slowly coming to an end. We see this in declining asset prices. Inflation, declining trust, high indebtedness, and other reasons lead to reduced returns or defaults.

The hard money now **becomes soft—emotional, and thus happy money**. And we become happy. Because today, we are not happy, as we chase financial returns and align ourselves with luxury goods and status symbols.

This new transformation of money has the following benefit: The social value of a person is raised and is no longer defined by their possession of material goods, but by what **emotional joy** they create for themselves and others. It is about a new togetherness rather than competition and self-profit. Success will no longer be measured by financial gain and wealth, but by satisfaction and positive emotions.

People will not accumulate material goods but will spread joy through generosity, care, and their abilities. Bonds between people could thus gain depth and meaning. **Trust would be the new "currency."** Today's money would be secondary. Emotional values like **empathy, compassion, joy, and satisfaction** would be the most valuable resources.

It is a mutual inspiration: we become happy when we handle money differently and see it grow, **and money becomes happy because we are happy**. Thus, it comes to us. We make each other happy. It's a restart of our money and life system.

We become like children. Children aren't happy because they have money. They are happy from within. And then they receive gifts (money and other presents). They use it to build a new world through play and watch it grow. They are delighted and happy. Money plays a secondary role for them. It is not heavy but light.

We also now see money differently: we transform our previous view of "money is heavy; it is associated with envy, jealousy, deceit" into money is light. It comes easily to us.

From today's heavy, dark, tainted, sorrowful money, we create "Happy Money." We imagine happy money flowing to us. We embrace it and love it—very much. We visualize this metaphor every day. And then **happy money flows to us**—first sparsely, then more and more.

We change our intention: no longer striving for more and more but being content with what we have. And using money for things that benefit everyone.
We have trust and believe in something greater: an invisible, universal energy supports us because our intention is good—for the benefit of Earth and humanity—serving the common good and not just (as before) ourselves and our ego.

This belief and trust are a new movement called **Money & Spirit**. It means that money comes from a great power once we have changed our thinking, altered our intentions, and developed trust. We can forget our previous actions, thoughts, and intentions regarding money and the destructive handling of it. The times of greed, envy, jealousy, deceit, manipulation, and corruption surrounding money are definitely over.

We bring money—gold—from heaven to earth. How? By letting the golden light—our intuition and inspiration—flow through us every day. This light makes us aware of what we need to tackle to create something new. We were born with gifts, and we can now use them to transform the disruptive world into a new, more beautiful one.

Happy Money is thus the new money energy. We develop a new attitude towards money: no more addiction to money, no more racing after money! And perhaps we sever the connection to the family, specifically the negative energies.

A friend shared the following example. Her father had a poor relationship with money. It slipped through his fingers. The money did not stay with him. And his daughter experienced the same thing as an adult. One day, she met an energy mentor. "You need to separate from your father's energy," she said.
And so, she did, saying to her father in her mind: "Your relationship with money is not my issue (my responsibility), but yours. It has nothing to do with me. I now free myself from this destructive energy." From that point on, money flowed to her. And it stayed with her. The money felt comfortable with her and multiplied. It loved the woman, and the woman loved the money.

And thus, an unhappy state became a happy one. My friend is very happy because she was able to heal other issues with this method as well. How did she manage it? By untangling connections with the family, in this case, money entanglements. We can untangle all connections: in the family, in work, in bad relationships, boring jobs, alcohol, and other problems.

But as mentioned earlier: we can erase our past from our memory. A new era has begun. We can view money as a means that now comes easily to us, that is golden, and that flows to us.

We can eliminate family and personal burdens today. The source and cause of our discomfort in emotional and monetary areas are found within our family history. This leads us to our roots and to the roots of our family, which may bring us to suffering, pain, and sorrow caused by the family.

On the path to a positive relationship with money, we learn to forgive. And we reconcile with our history. In the end, there is healing—of our ancestors, ourselves, and thus our connection to money.

For this, we can:

➠ Change our beliefs and conditioning.

➠ Let joy flow into our activities.

➠ Open our hearts.

➠ Let go of money and stop clinging to it.

➠ Use money for people and the earth to make them happy.

➠ Trust that money will flow back to us.

➠ Believe in the greater whole.

Through our transformation, money flows.

➠ Inner wealth becomes more important than outer wealth.

➠ Joy and lightness instead of greed, fear, and worry.

➠ Love instead of envy, resentment, and jealousy.

After this, we look at money with different eyes—with a new consciousness. The tree is planted! It represents us and gives us our stability. It's an amazing time. The old goes, and the new comes. A new epoch has begun.

And this is the way to HAPPY MONEY.

Money is love. Money is prosperity. Money is abundance. When we invest money in something that touches our heart, we experience the feeling of happiness. Then joy arises, and our fears disappear. And we see the investment grow. And we are grateful.

The new money makes everything bloom. And we will bloom too! Our money makes us flourish—our health, our family, our job, and so on. **We give money with joy, love, and gratitude. And we receive it back with joy, love, and gratitude**. And thus, the economy blooms. In this way, everything can bloom **with joy, with love, with gratitude, and with appreciation.**

Money is given to us for this purpose. When we act from the heart, money comes to us (automatically). Let it happen! Let us trust! Let us make greed for "more", as well as fear and worry, things of the past. **Let joy, light, and sunshine into our lives**!

Because human capital is not just "external gold"—money—but also our potential, talents, and creativity, our courage and trust, our morality, honesty, and transparency, as well as our joy and health. With this capital, we can always build something new.

Many people, due to their education, have pursued activities that are not necessarily connected to their hearts. They do things that bring no joy, that are not heart-centric. They do everything from the mind, as society, the family, school, and university have taught them. As a result, people have adopted beliefs that are no longer valid today.

Today we can trust ourselves: our talents, our creativity and competence, our intentions, and our intuition in the decisions we make or the paths we choose every day, even if something should go wrong. When people embrace this new awareness of themselves, they will become "rich." And then the money will come too.

Money comes to us effortlessly when we:
- APPRECIATE money
- View it as ENERGY that returns to us if we handle it well and benevolently (and not greedily, exploitatively, deceitfully)
- Use our HEART, LOVE, and SPIRIT
- Are OPEN and HONEST with ourselves and everyone
- Have JOY in what we do
- Do GOOD for others
- Invest money in GOOD THINGS
- SHARE money. Sharing = Healing
- Make PEACE with money, with ourselves, and with everyone.

Money is like a beloved baby. We embrace it, love it, and treat it with care.

With a new attitude—a new perspective—we can turn today's "heavy money" into happy money—HAPPY MONEY.

Trust is crucial. We have so far had trust in the system, as mentioned at the beginning: "The acceptance of money is based on people's trust in its value and its ability to function as a medium of exchange and store of value."

Now it is about our trust—not in the system (which is earthly) but in the greater whole. We are connected with everything—also with a higher dimension/entity (= the Spirit), with our true divine "Self." And from there comes money—in the form of the gifts and talents we brought to earth.

As children, we do not yet know our gifts and talents. But we unconsciously use them, are creative, and build or develop something. Money may also be involved, but the focus of the child is not on money. The child doesn't even know it. The focus is on what it wants to create. Money plays a secondary role.

In my book "The Happy Money," I write about the child whose heart is open and touched by the many beautiful things that appear in the child's world. Its imagination and creativity know no bounds. The child wants to build a new world. It starts by taking its savings to a nursery to buy a plant. It gives it water, love, and good energy. It watches the plant grow.
The family gives the child new money, and it buys a second plant. It also gives this plant water, love, and good thoughts. It watches it grow every day. And so, it builds a new world—a world made of nature, happy people, and happy money, where appreciation, love, and happiness are the new foundation of life.

And this is the transformation: instead of viewing money in adulthood as heavy and mishandling it, we go back to childhood and see money as playing a secondary role, but with great appreciation and love. Thus, Happy Money comes to us playfully.

8. Chapter: Happiness and Spirituality

We live in a visible and an invisible world. We recognize the visible one and believe the statements of scientists.

The invisible world is suspect to many people. We do not believe the messages expressed in this realm—at least, not until they are scientifically explained, proven, and physically tangible. And this is where opinions diverge. Some need scientific proof; others do not. They know from their past (past lives) and from their intuition that the invisible, scientifically unproven world is true and real.

We humans are beings of energy, composed of five percent consciousness. Ninety-five percent is the unconscious. Many believe that our five percent of knowledge is disproportionately significant, enabling us to display ego, arrogance, and know-it-all attitudes rather than practicing humility and wisdom.

Our physical body consists of energy centers, also called chakras. These centers form a communication system— comprising nerves and hormones. These converge in the seven chakras of the body.

Surrounding the physical body are light bodies, and these light bodies attract other people, as mentioned in the foreword. Today, we should let our light body shine in gold so that many people are drawn to us. **We should radiate joy and cheerfulness**. We should make those around us happy.

And we should meet others at eye level, not seeing them as subordinates or worshipers—radiating kindness.

"It needs just a smile to make other people happy."

However, when the nervous and hormonal systems are not in balance, a person lives in fear, fight, or flight. Their world becomes unsafe, leading to trauma, stress, and illness.

Shamans are experts in healing trauma. When they heal the body, they restore balance to the nervous and hormonal systems. By doing this, we avoid storing our traumas—in the vagus nerve, which connects the brain with every organ in the body. The vagus nerve is then realigned, and thus, we heal trauma.

Through this balance, we can also change people's consciousness—from materialism to inner values, from egoism to the common good, from "I" to "we," from a focus on money to a focus on happiness, and from our current patriarchal, masculine energy to a feminine one.

Ninety-five percent of all actions take place in the invisible field. It is an energy field that communicates with the quantum field. Shamans are at home in this field. They know how to deal with trauma. They hold the knowledge of ancient wisdom. They are the old wise ones.

We, too, can become wise. We can learn from the old wise ones. We can put aside our pride, our arrogance, and our sense of superiority.

And so, we come to happiness—a sense of joy whose source is not the external, not the material, but our inner values, our heart, and our soul (and thereby our psyche).

In this context: How can it be that a person, whose body cells are full of cancer, knowing they have only a few months left to live and that they will leave behind an 18-year-old son alone in the world, is still **full of joy, laughter, and positivity**?

I met this person in 2015 at the Hippocrates Health Institute in West Palm Beach, Florida, during my first visit to this institute. Jackie stood in the middle of the dining room—blonde, angelic, radiant, happy. She welcomed me without knowing who I was. She told her story. I was deeply impressed. Such suffering. Such fate. And then such joy. Such happiness. Such deep inner knowing. Such a divine presence.

Jackie Campisi was an ophthalmologist in Connecticut near New York, running a successful practice. Then she was diagnosed with spinal cancer. She went through a very tough time in her life. In the end, the cancer was defeated, her practice was lost, and her health insurance was canceled due to the high cost of cancer treatment.

She heard about the Hippocrates Health Institute in West Palm Beach and moved to Florida with her partner. She started working at this institute, helping cancer patients to see their world as hopeful and positive rather than sad and negative. She gave them **support, confidence, and zest for life**.

Then cancer returned. The doctors gave her one year to live. She remained cheerful, hopeful, and radiant all day long. I accompanied her and her partner for a long time.
At that time, I lived in Miami and frequently drove to Palm Beach to see her, to give her strength, to absorb her wisdom, and to experience her invisible connection to something greater—a source from which she drew daily. She was not religious, but there was a source that guided her and gave her strength, enabling her to inspire not only herself but others as well—bringing them **joy, happiness, and delight**.

After the year predicted by the doctors had passed, and she was still alive, an additional sense of happiness was born for her. She lived another year. But it became increasingly difficult as she lost her job at the institute, had no more money, and her body slowly declined. In the end, she received a stem cell transplant as a sponsorship, but it no longer helped. I had since returned to Hamburg, but I kept in touch with her frequently. And then she slowly passed away.

Two months later, I booked a flight to Miami to visit friends. What a surprise: I received the news that a memorial service for Jackie was to be held in West Palm Beach on the Sunday after my arrival. What a coincidence that this service was planned when I was to be in Miami. The organizers of the memorial service did not know that I had planned a trip to Miami. On that Sunday, I naturally drove to West Palm Beach and delivered the eulogy for Jackie Campisi.

It was a beautiful ceremony—full of lightness, joy, and gratitude for Jackie's messages to those **she gave strength, confidence, light, and love** to, as well as my heartfelt gratitude for having known Jackie—this angelic, almost divine being, who today floats above us in her invisibility, bringing her happiness to earth.

> *"Laughter is like a release—just as tears are.*
> *When I became a Buddhist,*
> *I learned, and finally understood, that the past, present,*
> *and future are one. Everything that has happened to me*
> *—the good and the bad—is a part of me.*
> *I have accepted it. And this acceptance makes me stronger."*
> Tina Turner

In September 2007, I gave a lecture at a prestigious Private Bank in Hamburg titled, "How to Bring the Gold of Heaven to Earth." The gold of heaven is also invisible. You can't touch it. But it is there. Gold is, on the one hand, our inner gold—our talents, potentials, and gifts that we bring to earth at birth. And on the other hand, it is the external gold—our money, which flows to us because of our gifts. Thus, it is our inner values that we materialize. And with that, to the topic: How do I bring the gold of heaven to earth?

9. Chapter: How to Bring the Gold of Heaven to Earth?

On September 17, 2007, I delivered the following lecture at the premises of the once-honorable private bank Sal. Oppenheim, in their Hamburg branch. Prior to this, I had an intuition—a premonition—that the 200-year-old private bank would not remain in its current form for much longer. And indeed, sometime later, the bank had to be taken over by Deutsche Bank due to imprudent and speculative dealings. Otherwise, it would have had to file for bankruptcy.

What a disgrace for a family that had managed this respectable bank for over seven generations. But, as described in this book, family members often endure fates that are not necessarily the result of their own actions but are caused by the deeds of their ancestors. They are born into these families because their soul has chosen this path and wishes to undergo specific experiences.

Incidentally, the day after my lecture, I was called to meet with the management. They informed me that they were not pleased with the lecture's content, as it did not promise monetary profit. On the other hand, the audience's feedback was very positive.
At the end of the lecture, a distinguished lady from Hamburg stood up to congratulate me on presenting such a complex topic in a concise and illustrative way, and she invited me on a journey

to India, where the topic of inner wealth and spirituality was being taught at a university. A few weeks later I traveled to India.

On October 5, 2007, I gave the same lecture at the Rotary Club Hamburg-Altona. It was well received by some Rotarians, but others were less enthusiastic.

A few months earlier, I had given a lecture on Latin America and concluded with the statement: "Many Latin Americans, particularly the indigenous people, have no material wealth but possess an inner treasure, expressed through their bright, joyful eyes and laughter. Here in Western Europe, I see people with great material wealth, but without laughter or bright, joyful eyes on their faces."

This statement didn't win me any friends either. The Rotarians looked away awkwardly.

Here is my lecture:

Ladies and Gentlemen, dear Friends!

Welcome to these wonderful rooms of Sal. Oppenheim.

First of all, I would like to thank the Private Bank Sal. Oppenheim and its Head of Northern Germany, Mr. von Hirschhausen, for allowing me to speak here today.

I am delighted to be able to present on a very special topic today:

"How to Bring the Gold of Heaven to Earth?"

Let me briefly introduce myself, outline the life of Michael H., a businessman from Latin America, and share with you my vision of TRUE WEALTH.

The purpose of this lecture is to create AWARENESS of the UNITY between inner and outer WEALTH.

1. Personal Introduction:

I am married, have a 13-year-old daughter and an 11-year-old son. I spent 15 years of my life as a banker in Latin America. Another 6 years in the USA. I worked for renowned German and Swiss banks. For many years now, I have been an independent advisor for banks.

Through my personal experiences and fates, I have embarked on a completely new path. And that is what I would like to tell you about today. I seek to create a **balance of wealth** for those willing to embrace it.

The value placed on money is "out of balance." It must be reduced from its overemphasized position to a reasonable level. **The focus should be on people and not on money, because money alone does not bring happiness**.

How should this happen? Idea: We could transform money into gold. **For gold represents both inner and outer wealth!**

Gold is not just a metal; it is also an energy—a spiritual force that we must learn to harness.

In this sense, the statement by the former President of Abu Dhabi, Sheikh Zayed bin Sultan Al Nahyan, should be understood:

"Wealth has no real value unless it serves the people."

2. Photo Selection

a) Wealthy, famous personalities (outer wealth)

As you can see, these are individuals who have amassed tremendous material wealth.

b) Happy, heartfelt people = love, joy, friendship, soul (inner wealth)

We all know these great men of wealth and can also see their inner suffering. We all know moments of happiness and love, and feel the deep longing for them.

Why do wealthy Europeans and Americans often have tense faces, full of worry and fear about their money?
Why do poor people have a happy smile on their faces?

What are true values?
What is outer wealth?
What is inner wealth?
How can I attain both?

How can money become GOLD?
What kind of gold is meant here?

We can only reach it if we do one thing:
We must take the spiritual path;
we must give soul to the money.

3. The Story of Michael H.

This WISDOM has been realized by some people, like the businessman Michael H., about whom I will briefly tell you now. Why him? Because Michael understood that only the UNITY of inner and outer WEALTH leads to HAPPINESS.

Michael H. was born in Hamburg in 1941. He came from humble beginnings. He completed an apprenticeship as an import-export merchant.
When he was 20, his LUCK began: he got an opportunity to work at a grocery chain in Latin America.

But soon after, Michael faced his first misfortune: the owners had been reckless with the finances, and the company went bankrupt.
Michael seized a new opportunity. He started a sugarcane plantation. But this endeavor also failed. A fire destroyed the entire plantation. He was left with high debts and no job.

What truly helped him through all these setbacks was his wife Marilu, whom he met shortly after arriving in Peru and married. She accompanied Michael on his life journey. She was always by his side—even in the darkest moments. She brought a ray of light to the darkness of his business situations. She always gave him COURAGE. When she looked at him with her warm, dark brown eyes, he knew he had to keep going.

And so, he managed to achieve a lot in his life. He became a successful entrepreneur in the shipping industry and built up a large fortune. But even on this path, he experienced ups and downs. He learned his life lessons.
He went through experiences that caused him deep pain. He was blackmailed and had to give a large part of his business profits to a government official for decades. He lived with the

constant fear of his family being kidnapped. For this reason, he had his children study abroad.
In all these situations, Marilu would smile at him with her warm eyes, as she was aware that one cannot control fate...

He became wise. He searched for the meaning of life, and he found it. He found his path in life, the one he was meant to walk on Earth. And that's what it is about on Earth: Everyone should find their path, and each person must walk it alone. But everyone is helped along the way. The helpful key is the inner attitude: "Have faith in God."

Today, when Michael looks out over the harbor from his apartment in Hamburg and reflects on his life, he feels proud of what he has created and feels very happy. His wife and four children fill his HEART. It is the BALANCE between material and inner VALUES. WEALTH has been created.
What truly matters to him in life is HAPPINESS, contentment, and family. And that cannot be paid for with MONEY.

Whoever creates this BALANCE is a happy, fulfilled person. Today, many are searching for HAPPINESS and MONEY. It lies on the street; it lies WITHIN US. We just have to be ready to receive it.

The story of Michael represents the life journey of many Germans abroad—but not only abroad.

It mirrors my own life journey. Michael touched on my themes when he said: the only thing that is of true WORTH are the comforting, gentle eyes of his wife.

This statement has an important spiritual component: through the eyes, we look into people's souls. And with souls like Marilu's, we find comfort and healing that truly helps. This is an universal law.

Why am I telling this story?
Michael's life mirrors the LIFE OF US ALL: there are ups and downs. A LIFE never runs in a straight line. But after every "down" comes an "up."
Michael never gives up; he always draws STRENGTH and optimism to start anew. I experienced the same resilience in the USA: Americans also always start over after a setback. And we Germans? After a professional failure, many Germans lose hope.

I, too, have walked through valleys and felt despair. I also struggled with this doubt for a long time. Now I am climbing the mountain again. I have picked myself up and am therefore able to help others in difficult situations (bankruptcies/deaths) to SEE THE LIGHT.

In summary, what has touched me?

- Michael's awakening. His expanded awareness.
 His resilience and perseverance.

- His hard work and his LOVE and DEVOTION to his
 work.
 Through this, the money came to him.

- The emphasis of his life priorities:
 money is not the most important thing for Michael,
 but rather his love for his wife and children.

- His wife, who always encourages him, gives him
 strength, and supports him, who loves unconditionally.

4. **My Vision for Money - Gold**
 And here we are at my vision of making the world a
 better place. I distinguish between "inner wealth" and
 "outer wealth."

 What is inner wealth? Of course: the HEART, LOVE, the
 FEELING of being happy!

 Inner wealth means
- becoming aware and taking personal responsibility.

Then we are able to create balance between the poles, which represent the feminine and masculine on Earth. We come to the center.

This is the basic prerequisite for dealing with what we are discussing here today, namely MONEY, in a meaningful and satisfying way.

How I see it:

Money is merely the neutral, flowing energy between two poles—the means.

In this awareness, money creates balance, and then money brings happiness.

I create awareness of unity in my clients and awareness of all-encompassing love. This creates a feeling of contentment and happiness. The path there leads through spirituality. And the means to accomplish this come through money.

I connect financial ventures (the handling of money) with spirituality.

God - Gold - Money.

The Scale Exercise:

I want to show you the balance between inner and outer wealth with a small exercise.
On the left side of the scale, we place **houses, cars, and yachts**.
On the right is the inner wealth: **love, joy, and talents**.
You see, the BALANCE is missing.
How can we create balance? We create balance by adding pieces of gold to the side of love and joy. Thus, outer wealth is balanced and comes into harmony.

GOLD actually represents outer wealth.
However, the gold on the right side represents inner wealth – the intangible. This also includes spirituality - the belief and the faith in something higher. We may fill this part in people. Their focus has been on the material, physical side so far. By giving people JOY, HAPPINESS, LIGHTNESS, and SPIRIT, we create a balance between material values and inner values.

And with this **Spirit, Joy, and Love**, we invest the ideal gold into earthly projects. And these new projects, in turn, bring us back **Joy and Happiness**.

To sum it up:

Inner wealth (= Gold vision) means:

1. Coming into SELF-LOVE, SELF-WORTH.

2. To VALUE oneself, to be RICH, SUCCESSFUL, and PROSPEROUS.

3. To work with LOVE, that is, with the HEART. (Then money comes automatically.)

4. To TRUST IN GOD.

5. To listen to the INNER VOICE (= intuition).

6. To live CONSCIOUSLY. To become aware of one's gifts/talents.

7. To live in the NOW, not in the PAST or the FUTURE.

8. To take PERSONAL RESPONSIBILITY: "Trust yourself!"

9. To follow one's OWN PATH and live one's OWN TRUTH.

10. To see the MEANING of LIFE in everything and to see all experiences, things, and people POSITIVELY. *Everything is as it should be. Therefore, do not question everything. Everything has its purpose. There are no coincidences.*

11. To acknowledge the changes of "Ups & Downs." (Everything on Earth goes up and down: positive/negative, sun/moon, day/night, rain/sun, yin/yang, etc.)

12. To create BALANCE! To come to the CENTER! (That means developing a balance between feminine and masculine energy. The same applies to MONEY: there must always be balance.)

13. To come to the CENTER, to develop the DIVINE POINT.

14. Not to JUDGE and not to CONDEMN!

15. To have PATIENCE and remain CALM. Not to be impatient! "Not as I will, but as YOU will."

16. To engrave a GUIDING PRINCIPLE: "Everything and everyone brings me happiness now!"

Outer Wealth - How Can I Increase Outer Wealth (= Money Vision)?

You all know what outer wealth means. The most important thing for outer wealth is the proper, meaningful investment. **Use money wisely, manage it well and wisely, and handle it with care**: this is the responsibility of every person, every entrepreneur, every banker, and asset manager. But there are only a few wise investors.

Now, my goal is to use outer wealth well and meaningfully for the benefit of all. Because it is the PERSON who does something GOOD or BAD with MONEY.
Money remains neutral, whether it is in Germany, Switzerland, or Luxembourg.
So, we should use MONEY well, that is, POSITIVELY. We should handle it carefully. We should appreciate it and treat it with LOVE. Then it develops positively. That is the secret of success that I am concerned with.

The same applies to investments. We should invest in assets with understanding, respect, and love. We should handle investments well and put positive energy into them, that is, we should GIVE SOUL to and BLESS the investments.
Then they develop positively. Because investments are not living beings like humans or animals. They have no SOUL. But we humans have a SOUL. And when we use our MONEY with HEART and LOVE, whether it is buying a house, a car, a bond, or

a stock, when we love it with our HEART, then it develops positively because we have GIVEN SOUL to what we have acquired.

I must have no resentments. And I must have PATIENCE: not, my GOD, as I will, but as YOU WILL.

If you love your MONEY and invest it with devotion and LOVE in things that are close to your HEART, then it will be profitable. However, if you invest your money solely to make more of it and otherwise disregard the matter, it will come to nothing. This means, it is not enough to invest your money in something and think that everything is now safe and it will multiply. It is important to be actively involved, even spiritually. You should establish an inner connection to YOUR investments. Put all the positivity of your being into the business. Then it multiplies and benefits everyone. So, invest not only with the MIND but also with the HEART.

Some people have already understood how to handle MONEY correctly: One way to handle outer wealth well is to donate it or leave it to foundations, museums, etc. In this way, they do something GOOD with it. This allows GOOD to flow back to these people.

And one more thing is important to remember: **Money is transient**. We earn it in life, and then we leave it to others. Money is only lent to us in life. We should view MONEY as if it were lent to us. Everything we buy with it is a loan.

Warren Buffet will not leave his fortune to his children but will donate it for the benefit of the general public. Because, as he says: the money was only lent to him. He gives it back for good causes.

Alfred Nobel and many others have done the same: they used MONEY for the benefit of the general public.

Outer Wealth (= Gold Vision) means:

1. Let MONEY flow.

2. Give MONEY the RIGHT VALUE. *(There is nothing negative about money. You do not need to fear money will be lost, earn too little return, be offshore, etc.)*

3. LOVE MONEY and everything acquired with it.

4. HANDLE MONEY CONSCIOUSLY.

5. GAIN KNOWLEDGE (and wisdom) of capital investments and their RISKS. *(Strengthen financial knowledge, create financial education! Set up investments so that they serve people, see money as a "loan," create "abundance," etc.)*

5. And now my answer to the question of the beginning:

"How do I Bring the Gold of Heaven to Earth?"

I help in my work to find inner wealth, that is, to perceive happiness and contentment.

"A fulfilled life is not the result of fulfilling all wishes.
It is the fruit of a heart filled with love."

How do I attain this "heart filled with love,"
independent of financial possessions?
The key is to soften the hardness of the heart.

I see GOLD in heaven and bring it to YOU on earth by giving blessings. It is my HEARTFELT wish that YOU are HAPPY, both inwardly and outwardly. I want to give people MONEY and GOLD, inner and outer wealth!

And in this context, I would like to conclude by thanking Sal. Oppenheim bank. This house has shown a great heart to its friends, acquaintances, and family for seven generations—even in difficult times. Of course, a bank must also act according to economic principles.

For many years, however, we have seen only the purely commercial side of all banks. The human side has long been lost. But the private bank Sal. Oppenheim has never forgotten this human side and continues to cultivate it strongly. It maintains the tradition of holding on to old values, to human values, and does not think about short-term profits but cares about long-term customer relationships. And thus, it stands out for its stability.

And that is the most important thing in our current short-term thinking era. Because markets go up and down. The most important thing is the preservation and long-term increase of wealth. And that is one of the focuses of the bank. I am happy to work with Sal. Oppenheim in the future.

And so, I conclude with the words of James D. Wolfensohn, ex-President of the World Bank Group, which he spoke at the annual meeting of the World Bank in Dubai in 2003, because these words express what is close to my heart:

"Mr. Chairman: I do not speak as a dreamer or a philosopher.
Like all of you, I too have a family and worry about their future.
We have the **knowledge** to make a difference.
We have the **resources** to make a difference.
We have the **courage** to make a difference.
We must act now to make a difference."

James D. Wolfensohn, Ex-President of the World Bank
"The future means a growing imbalance between people,
natural resources, and the environment. If we act today,
we can prevent these imbalances and set the world
on a better future course. If we do not act,
we will leave our children with greater problems."

*"The highest goal of capital is not to make money,
but to use money to improve life."*
Henry Ford

I am pleased to build a new financial world with you.
Thank you very much for your attention!

How do I bring the gold of heaven to earth?
The gold represents joy, love, and happiness.

Today, I would answer: I bring people their inner gold to earth—their true essence, their true purpose, their awakening—as well as cheerfulness, happiness, and sunshine. I am the bridge between heaven and earth.

Radiant, golden LIGHT flows to people. Golden LIGHT shines around them. This fills them with LOVE. They feel secure. They feel good. They are happy. A deeply felt HAPPINESS and JOY surrounds them. They are touched by this light. It fills their HEARTS. They feel LOVE and the connection to something greater—the universal energy.
They feel happy, understood, and have arrived in their hearts. Full of joy, they embrace their family, friends, neighbors, and community.

And this mood is contagious. Others come and want to see what is happening here: a great transformation—from depression, fear, and suffering to the opening of hearts, receiving golden light, and feeling joy and happiness.

Conclusion

We enter happiness by directing our attention...
- Back to childhood: letting curiosity, enthusiasm, creativity, emotions flow freely.
- Not clinging to the old. Letting go.
- Connecting with the greater whole and letting ourselves be guided.
- Shifting our perspective: seeing our world with joy, not with worries.
- Giving others a smile. Then smiles come back.
- Gratitude and forgiveness.

Then we reach the state of happiness – cheerfulness – playfulness – inner wealth – inner contentment – inner values – peace – freedom – carefreeness – serenity – mental health.

And this is the most important thing in life: mental health and contentment. Yet many people lack contentment and happiness. They are focused on material values instead of inner values.
And they are afraid – of change. They cling to the old – the material.

Message
When we are content within, we don't need to accumulate so much possession outwardly. And then we can use money for other things, like helping others to find joy or independence, etc.

The great challenge is **to come into silence** and listen within (and discover our soul's/life's path). So far, we have only used our intellect. But the world has changed.
We must learn not to give our mind too much space.
We must welcome a higher consciousness. It is energy.

Money is part of our life. Money is also energy. Yet it is one of the great obstacles to achieving happiness. Because we have a poor relationship with money; we worry and fear; we have too little or too much of it, etc.
Money wants to be honored, loved, and recognized. Money wants to be seen with higher consciousness, with a higher dimension/instance.

Metaphor

Imagine money could hear, feel, and talk (like a human). What would money hear? It would hear what you want to do with it, what you want to use it for.
And what would it feel? It feels whether it is being used well or badly. We humans feel when we are treated poorly. What if money could also feel this?
When you use money for something positive, money feels good.
But if you trade money for something negative (fast food, alcohol, cigarettes), does the money feel good then? What experiences have you had?
And if money could talk! Wow! What a new realization.

Message

If we handle money well and use it wisely, joy and health come forth = cause - effect (and not fear, worry, guilt, depression). Everything is energy: people, water, money, love. Everything must flow. If it doesn't flow, there's congestion. And then illness arises.

Message

View everything with love. Open your heart. Give appreciation: to life, love, people, nature, and money. And treat everything well!

And where does water, we humans, money come from? Everything comes from the universe to Earth. Money too. We practically bring it with us at birth, since we are born with talents and potentials that we later convert into money.

Money comes to us easily when we
- APPRECIATE money
- see it as ENERGY that returns to us if we handle it well and benevolently (and not with greed, exploitation, fraud)
- use our HEART, LOVE, and SPIRIT
- are OPEN and HONEST with ourselves and everyone else
- have JOY in what we do
- do GOOD for others
- invest money in GOOD THINGS
- SHARE money
- make PEACE with money, with ourselves, and with everyone else.

Money is like a beloved baby. We hold it in our arms, love it, and take good care of it.

The following steps are very important: **have trust** (in everything). Trust the flow of money/business! Do not fear. This is the greatest hurdle. Because people are afraid, they hold on to it and prepare for bad times. When we are surrounded by fear, we will always let money control our lives.
However, if we are in trust, we can let go.

How do we gain trust?
1. Resolve entanglements with family, partner, job, etc.
2. Trust in us: I am not afraid that something will go wrong.
3. Trust in the greater whole – the higher dimension = Spirit.

Make peace – with ourselves with our family members, and with money.
We carry many wounds within us – wounds that come from our family/ancestors and our childhood.
We must understand that our parents and grandparents also suffered and carried these wounds. Whatever happened in our childhood: our parents and grandparents also endured fates.
And we carry these in our system (into old age). They need to be healed. We must let go of them, e.g., emotional wounds like not being seen, being left alone, emotional absence of the mother/father, not being loved, etc.

These deep-seated feelings of abandonment can continue into adulthood. Some want nothing to do with their family; others start drinking, take drugs, or work a lot to avoid thinking about it. How we love, how we struggle in our relationships – all this is connected to our childhood.

We do not have to repeat the patterns that shaped our childhood. We can overcome our traumas. We can heal ourselves – all on our own.

Making peace involves forgiveness – reconciliation.
We must make peace with ourselves, our parents, and ancestors. We must forgive them and reconcile with them.

Exercise: Imagine taking yourself in your arms, holding yourself tightly, forgiving and reconciling with yourself. Now imagine taking your mother in your arms, holding her, forgiving and reconciling with her.
Do the same with your father.

We must **give thanks** – thank ourselves for the experience we had with our parents. That is healing! We forgive ourselves for going down an unwholesome path in life and for making shady deals. Then we forgive everyone we have harmed – materially and emotionally.
And then we forgive our parents, through whom we unconsciously came into this money topic.

When we plant a tree, start a new project, find a new love, etc. and we give a lot of heart, love, and spirit to the root/ground, then the tree, the plant, the project, the investment, the money grows and blossoms. **Because with our higher consciousness, everything grows where we put it.**

The return will be a holistic one, not only material but also immaterial: **joy in life, health, joy, enthusiasm, ease, purpose in life.**
And as we laugh and rejoice, money wants to laugh too.

It's about growing together
of inner and outer VALUES
of the inner and outer
of the material and the spiritual
of male and female energy
of the individual and society
of the left and right brain hemispheres.

Thus, a balance (Yin/Yang) is established. And thus, equilibrium is created: within people and among people. Through growth, people reach higher consciousness.

Today begins the time to connect **the material with the immaterial**. Thus, we gain both: **money and inner health**. We open our hearts.

And we give our life and money appreciation. We, as well as money, want to be "seen" and "acknowledged" – perceived as energy. Then it flows to us – manifold.

The goal or result of our transformation and new perspective is: **HAPPINESS, JOY, MEANING, CONTENTMENT, and thus HEALTH.**

Closing exercise: GOLD falls from the SKY

Imagine gold falling from the sky. See the gold coins falling from the sky. This divine gold represents **joy of life, bliss, cheerfulness, and love**. Pick up the coins slowly and gently. Feel the gold. It is warm. It is loving. It is heartfelt. Press it to your heart!

Appendix (Text by ChatGPT 4.0)

I. Our shared journey of transformation

To continue on this journey of transformation: We need to understand that our subconscious mind is shaped by past experiences and emotions, many of which we may not even be aware of. By bringing these hidden elements to the surface and processing them, we can begin to free ourselves from the patterns that limit us.

Meditation, mindfulness, and practices that encourage self-reflection are powerful tools for this journey. By calming the mind, we can access the deeper layers of our consciousness, allowing us to observe and eventually release the emotions that have been stored there.

The Role of Forgiveness and Gratitude

Forgiveness is not about condoning the actions of others; it is about freeing ourselves from the emotional weight that we carry. When we forgive, we release the energy tied up in past grievances, creating space for new, positive energy to flow in.

Gratitude, on the other hand, shifts our focus from what is lacking to what is already present and abundant in our lives. It is a practice that elevates our vibration and aligns us with the energy of love and abundance.

Reconnecting with Our Inner Child

To truly heal, we must reconnect with our inner child—the part of us that is pure, creative, and filled with wonder. This reconnection allows us to experience life with a sense of playfulness and joy, unburdened by the fears and expectations that have accumulated over time. By nurturing our inner child, we can rediscover the simple joys of life and cultivate a sense of lightness and freedom.

Living in the Present Moment

The present moment is the only place where true change can occur. When we dwell on the past, we keep old wounds open. When we worry about the future, we create anxiety. By focusing on the present, we can fully experience life as it is, without the distortions of past pain or future fears. This presence allows us to respond to life with clarity, compassion, and creativity.

Embracing the Journey

The journey to happiness and fulfillment is not a straight path. It is filled with ups and downs, moments of clarity, and times of confusion. The key is to embrace the journey with an open heart, trusting that every experience is part of our growth. By letting go of the need for perfection and allowing ourselves to be human, we create space for joy, connection, and true transformation.

In the end, happiness is not something we achieve; it is something we become. It is the result of living authentically, loving deeply, and embracing each moment as it comes. As we continue to heal and grow, we become beacons of light, spreading joy and positivity to those around us.

Let us walk this path together, supporting one another as we transform fear into love, and limitation into freedom.

Cultivating Inner Strength

To continue our journey of transformation, it is essential to cultivate inner strength. Inner strength is the ability to stay grounded and resilient in the face of life's challenges. It involves trusting ourselves, building self-discipline, and developing a mindset that sees obstacles as opportunities for growth. By cultivating inner strength, we can face our fears head-on, knowing that we have the power to overcome them.

The Power of Self-Love

Self-love is the foundation of a fulfilling and joyful life. It means accepting ourselves as we are, without judgment or criticism. When we love ourselves, we create an internal environment of safety and acceptance, which allows us to thrive.

Self-love also means setting healthy boundaries, prioritizing our well-being, and treating ourselves with the same kindness and compassion that we offer to others. By embracing self-love, we become our own source of support and happiness.

Creating Meaningful Connections

Human beings are social creatures, and meaningful connections are vital to our happiness. By cultivating relationships based on authenticity, empathy, and mutual support, we create a network of love and understanding that nourishes our soul.

True connection happens when we allow ourselves to be vulnerable, share our true selves, and listen deeply to others. These connections remind us that we are not alone and that we are all part of something greater.

Embodying Joy and Lightness

Joy and lightness are states of being that arise when we let go of the burdens we carry and allow ourselves to simply be. To embody joy, we must prioritize activities that bring us pleasure and fulfillment, whether it's spending time in nature, engaging in creative pursuits, or simply laughing with friends. Lightness comes from releasing the need to control everything and embracing the flow of life. By embodying joy and lightness, we inspire others to do the same and contribute to a more joyful world.

The Ripple Effect of Personal Transformation

Our personal transformation does not only impact us; it creates a ripple effect that touches everyone around us. When we heal ourselves, we contribute to the healing of our families, communities, and the world.

Our energy, thoughts, and actions influence those we come into contact with, and by embodying love, compassion, and authenticity, we inspire others to embark on their own journeys of transformation. Together, we can create a world where happiness, peace, and connection are the norm.

Continuing the Practice

Transformation is an ongoing process that requires consistent practice and dedication. It involves daily choices to align with love, release fear, and cultivate joy. Some practices that support this journey include meditation, journaling, spending time in nature, practicing gratitude, and engaging in acts of kindness.

By making these practices a regular part of our lives, we reinforce our commitment to growth and create lasting change.

Let us remember that we are all on this journey together. By supporting one another, sharing our experiences, and holding space for each other's growth, we create a community of transformation.

Let us continue to walk this path with courage, love, and an open heart, knowing that the journey itself is the destination, and that happiness is found in each step we take.

Final Thoughts

Happiness is not a destination but a way of being. It is the result of living in alignment with our true selves, embracing our emotions, and cultivating love and compassion for ourselves and others.

By letting go of what no longer serves us and stepping into our power, we can create a life filled with joy, purpose, and fulfillment. Let us commit to this journey of transformation, knowing that each moment offers us the opportunity to grow, heal, and experience the beauty of life in its fullness.

II. What do you understand by "Money & Spirit"?

"Money & Spirit" refers to the relationship between financial resources and a person's spiritual or inner values. It explores how money and material resources can be aligned with deeper, immaterial aspects of life—such as meaning, ethics, happiness, and fulfillment. Here are some central themes often discussed in this context:

Money as a flow of energy

In spiritual traditions, money is sometimes viewed as a form of energy that should flow and be shared. The goal is to develop a harmonious relationship with money, in which it is neither seen as the sole objective nor as an enemy, but as a tool that can be put in service of a greater spiritual purpose.

Mindfulness in dealing with money

"Money & Spirit" emphasizes the importance of being mindful and conscious in handling money. This means being aware of one's values and priorities and ensuring that the way one earns, spends, saves, or invests money aligns with those values. It asks the question: Does the use of money support my personal and spiritual growth?

Ethics and financial decisions

This concept also encompasses the ethical aspects of money. It asks questions such as: Is my money earned or invested in a way that aligns with my ethical principles? For example, one might consider whether they are investing in ethical companies or using their money for purposes that have a positive societal impact.

Freedom from material attachments

Many spiritual teachings emphasize that material goods and the desire for wealth should not be the ultimate goal in life. "Money & Spirit" explores how one can use money without being attached to it or seeing it as a source of self-worth or happiness. It is about balancing financial security with inner freedom.

Generosity and sharing

Generosity and the sharing of wealth are central themes in the relationship between money and spirituality. It is often stressed that true spiritual growth lies in the ability to support others and use material resources to foster the well-being of the community.

Abundance vs. scarcity

Another important concept is the distinction between a "scarcity mindset" (the belief that there is never enough) and an "abundance mindset" (the belief that the universe has enough resources for everyone). "Money & Spirit" encourages people to develop an abundance mindset, where one feels rich even if they don't possess much, because they trust in life and their own abilities.

In summary, "Money & Spirit" examines the deeper meaning of money in human life and how one can find a healthy, ethical, and spiritually fulfilling way of dealing with it. It is an approach that does not view money as something purely material or worldly, but as something deeply connected to a person's values, beliefs, and goals.